Grades 4–6

Problem Parade

Dale Seymour

DALE SEYMOUR PUBLICATIONS

Illustrations: Bob Larsen
Cover art: Julie Peterson

ISBN 0-86651-206-3
Order number DS01425

DALE
SEYMOUR
PUBLICATIONS
P.O. BOX 10888
PALO ALTO, CA 94303

11 12 13 14 16 17-MA-95

CONTENTS

INTRODUCTION

Problem Parade is a collection of 16 sets of problems for students in grades 4–6. Each set consists of three related problems, including one main problem, a warm-up problem that eases students into the concepts they will work with in the main problem, and an extension problem that leads the students to explore more difficult but related concepts.

Accompanying the problem book are 16 posters that display each of the main problems. These posters are spiral-bound in a calendar-style format with full-color illustrations. You may use these posters alone or with the corresponding worksheets in this book. The *Problem Parade* book itself may be used independently of the posters.

About the book

Each of the 48 problems appears in this book on a separate reproducible worksheet page, with space allowed for students to work out their solutions. You may duplicate the pages and distribute them as in-class assignments or as homework.

On the back of each student worksheet page is a discussion of the problem for the teacher, including the answer to the problem, points of interest about the problem, hints to help the students get started, an explanatory solution (where appropriate), and ways you might extend the problem into more difficult challenges.

Using the problems

Problems are arranged in general order of difficulty, although this will vary according to the background and problem-solving experience of your students. In any case, there is no required order for using the 16 sets of problems; simply choose those sets that best suit your students' learning situation. Within each set of problems, however, it is best to assign the warm-up problem first, then the main problem, and finally the extension problem.

In some cases you may want to use the warm-up problem for class discussion, then assign the main problem for independent work. Remember that student success is essential in the early stages of problem solving; some of these problems are quite difficult, and the time you spend on preparation may be critical to that success.

These problems are not the sort that can necessarily be solved in one sitting. Sometimes you may spend as much as a week on a single problem, letting students discover what they can and talking over what they've learned.

Focus on problem-solving strategies

The problems in this book are intended to help you concentrate on the development of students' *problem-solving* skills, so the emphasis is always on solution strategies rather than on computational practice. In fact, the math involved is generally quite simple. The use of calculators for any lengthy computation is to be encouraged. In these problems, students will be using mathematical skills they already have, but in new and sometimes exciting ways.

Different problems will require different strategies; often a problem can be solved in more than one way. Some of the strategies that students may find helpful are these:

Look for a pattern.
Guess and test.
Use logical reasoning.
Draw a picture.
Make an organized list.
Make a table or a diagram.
Use objects as models or act out the problem.
Work backwards.
Solve a simpler problem of the same sort.

Suggestions for teaching problem solving

Problem solving should be a part of every student's daily work in math. Try to allow from ten to fifteen minutes *every day* for discussion and work on problems. Few if any of the problems in this book are simple enough to be completed in a single ten-minute session, but that is as it should be. Such a schedule gives students time to think about the problem a bit, then leave it alone for a while and come back later with fresh ideas.

Here are some essential points about teaching problem solving:

Be actively involved with every problem.   You can't teach problem solving unless you are personally involved with it. Before assigning a problem to the class, *work it yourself*. What things need to be clarified, defined? What are possible approaches? What difficulties will students have? How does the problem tie into other work that students have done? What related problems does it suggest? Working the problem yourself, *without looking at the answer first*, will give you a much better feeling for what's going on, and will help you anticipate difficulties that students may encounter.

Define the problem.   Carefully discuss the *intent* of each new problem when you introduce it. Read the problem along with the class and invite questions. Taking care that students understand what a problem is asking is essential to their success.

Allow students to devise their own plans.   Different approaches to a problem are always possible, depending on the insights and skills of each student. Plan to discuss later the different ways that students tackled a problem; this can be illuminating to the class and teacher alike.

Suggest looking for simpler problems.   When students seem overwhelmed by a problem, urge them to look for a way they might simplify it. For example, you might suggest that they set up the same problem using easier numbers. This approach can sometimes make the strategies for solution a lot clearer.

Encourage written records of work.   Suggest that students make notes as they work on a problem. They should keep track of all their attempts, failures as well as successes. Lists, diagrams, pictures, and other problem-solving aids, even if they seem to lead nowhere, may trigger new ideas when the student returns to the problem later.

Answer questions with questions.   Don't give free information. Students must learn to think and reason through solutions themselves. Additionally, request that faster students keep their solutions to themselves, so that they don't deprive their peers of the thrill of discovery.

Take time.   Give students plenty of time to work with a problem and explore the different possible approaches. Afterwards, carry discussions to their fullest. Often this detailed after-the-fact analysis of the problem will constitute your most valuable teaching time.

Help students articulate general principles.   In many cases, students will have a feeling for the solution to a problem, but may be unable to say exactly what needs to be done, or even how they actually solved it. Help them learn to express general principles that emerge from the problems.

Solving a problem may not always be fun; sometimes it is hard work. But the pleasure in reaching a successful solution generally makes the effort worthwhile. Problem solving can be a rich and satisfying facet of mathematics. Let your students discover its rewards.

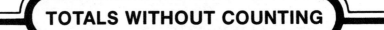

TOTALS WITHOUT COUNTING

Find the total number of dots in each figure. Use addition, multiplication, and subtraction to find your answer.

1. Do Not Count each one.
2. Show your thinking

1. [figure of dots]

2. [figure of dots]

3. [figure of dots]

4. [figure of dots]

5. [figure of dots]

6. [figure of dots]

TOTALS WITHOUT COUNTING

Answers
1. 50   4. 272
2. 180   5. 183
3. 215   6. 240

About the Problem

This kind of problem is designed to show students that multiplication is a more powerful tool than addition. Students may be less fearful of new concepts in math if they are reminded that new tools make the problem-solving task easier. Students also have a chance to see that there is more than one approach to a problem.

Getting Started

Remind students not to count each dot.

Rectangular arrays may obviously bring multiplication to mind.

Consider nonrectangular arrays as multistep problems; that is, break the problem into smaller parts. Encourage students to draw on the dot diagrams to help them visualize parts of the problem.

Solutions

1. A diagram 5 dots by 10 dots could be thought of as $5 \times 10 = 50$ or $10 \times 5 = 50$.
2. $15 \times 12 = 180$ or $12 \times 15 = 180$
3. $(12 \times 15) + (5 \times 7) = 180 + 35 = 215$ (sum of two rectangular arrays)
   Some might see the diagram as a rectangle with a section out of it, using subtraction instead of addition:
   $(12 \times 22) - (7 \times 7) = 264 - 49 = 215$
4. Addition approach:
   $(10 \times 16) + (6 \times 8) + (4 \times 16) = 160 + 48 + 64 = 272$
   Subtraction approach:
   $(22 \times 16) - (5 \times 8) - (5 \times 8) = 352 - 40 - 40 = 272$
5. Addition approach:
   $(9 \times 11) + (2 \times 5) + (6 \times 5) + (4 \times 11) = 99 + 10 + 30 + 44 = 183$
   Subtraction approach:
   $(18 \times 11) - (5 \times 3) = 198 - 15 = 183$
6. Combined addition and subtraction approach:
   $(17 \times 14) - (2 \times 14) + (5 \times 6) = 238 - 28 + 30 = 240$

Going Beyond

Some class discussion on "What is the best (easiest) approach to each solution?" might pay dividends.

Ask students if they can think of some real-world situations where using these approaches would lead to quick solutions. Finding the seating capacities of stadiums, theaters, or auditoriums are good examples.

Ask students to create some of their own problems of this type. Graph paper or dot paper would be helpful.

COUNTING STARS

Find the total number of stars shown. Don't count each star.
Use the patterns to find shortcuts.

COUNTING STARS

Answer   1980 stars

About the Problem

Mathematics has often been defined as "the study of patterns." The sooner that students become pattern-conscious, the better. This problem, like its warm-up, was designed to show students how ridiculous it would be to count every star. We can see that every row contains the same number of stars, as does every column. The student should see this as a multiplication problem rather than a counting problem.

The spaces between the rows and columns are included to encourage students to consider their effect on the problem. If there were no spaces, students would simply have to count the number of rows, then the number of columns, and multiply the two. The spaces may slow the students down and suggest another approach. That is, students may recognize a pattern of 1 + 2 + 3 + 4 + 5 + . . . rows and columns, and realize that adding could replace counting.

Getting Started

The problem is sufficiently easy that no hints should be necessary.

Solution

There are 1 + 2 + 3 + 4 + 5 + 6 + 7 + 8, or 36, rows of stars. In this case, even though there is a pattern, it may be faster for the student to count the 36 rows one by one rather than adding the first 8 numbers. The same is true with the 1 + 2 + 3 + 4 + 5 + 6 + 7 + 8 + 9 + 10, or 55, columns.

If students did use the pattern and have already found that 1 + 2 + 3 + 4 + 5 + 6 + 7 + 8 = 36, they could simply add 9 + 10 to the 36 to get 55.

The answer 1980, which students obtain by multiplying 36 times 55, is too many stars to count individually with any ease. Students should now understand how multiplication helps them "count without counting."

Going Beyond

The principles demonstrated by this problem can be extended to many real-world problems involving estimation of large quantities. For example:

If MacDougal's sells 3500 hamburgers a day, approximately how many would they sell in one year?

A large department store is about 100 meters long and 80 meters wide. How many floor tiles 25 cm × 25 cm are needed to cover each level of flooring?

Ask students to bring in pictures of rectangular arrays of objects. Have them write problems about the pictures.

All the shapes shown below were made with cubes. How many cubes were used for each?

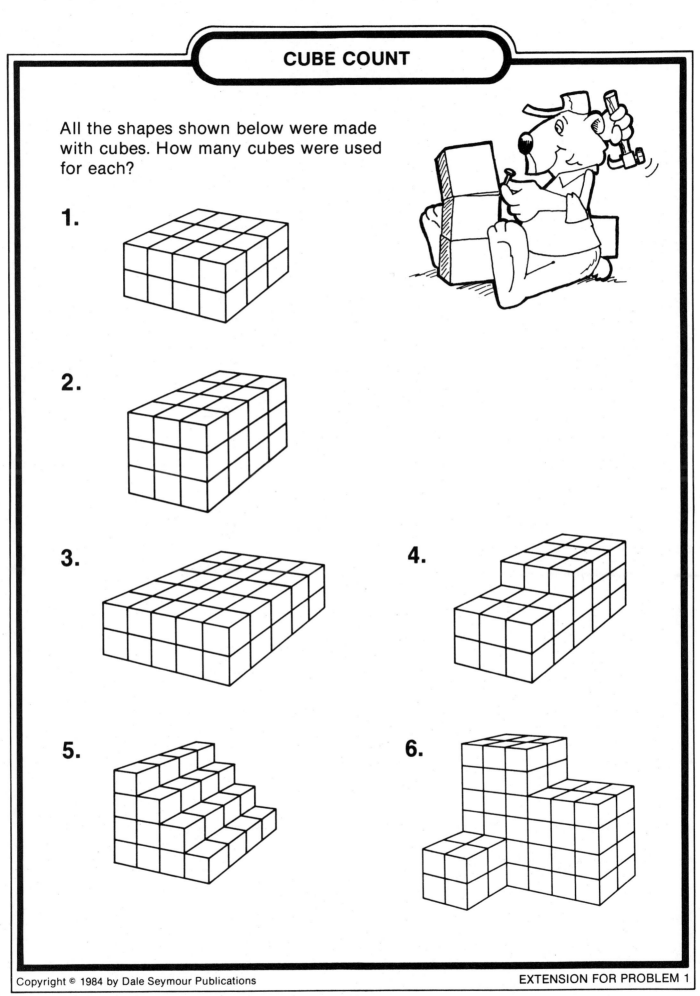

1.

2.

3.

4.

5.

6.

EXTENSION FOR PROBLEM 1

CUBE COUNT

Answers 1. 24   4. 39
           2. 36   5. 40
           3. 50   6. 68

About the Problem

This is an extension of the two-dimensional pattern problems that precede it. It is also a readiness activity for understanding the concept of volume.

When the solid shown is not a rectangular prism, students need to visualize the figure as two or more rectangular prisms—just as they saw nonrectangular dot arrays as two or more separate parts. With three-dimensional problems, though, they will be less likely to use subtraction than they were in the two-dimensional examples.

Getting Started

You may need to explain to students that there are no tricks. The walls they can't see are straight and complete.

Younger and less able students who have trouble visualizing may need to actually build these models to solve the problem.

Solutions

Ask students to give more than a number for their answers. Ask them to write out the expression that gave them the answer.

1. $2 \times 3 \times 4 = 24$
2. $3 \times 3 \times 4 = 36$
3. $2 \times 5 \times 5 = 50$
4. $(3 \times 3 \times 3) + (2 \times 2 \times 3) = 27 + 12 = 39$
5. $(1 \times 4) + (2 \times 4) + (3 \times 4) + (4 \times 4) = 4 + 8 + 12 + 16 = 40$
6. $(2 \times 2 \times 2) + (2 \times 2 \times 3) + (2 \times 4 \times 6) = 8 + 2 + 48 = 68$

This is a good time to reinforce the commutative and associative properties of multiplication, as follows:

commutative property of multiplication—The order of the numbers being multiplied doesn't matter.

  $a \times b = b \times a$

associative property of multiplication—When multiplying three or more numbers, it doesn't matter which numbers are multiplied first.

  $(a \times b \times c) = a \times (b \times c) = (a \times b) \times c$

Going Beyond

Problem 5 is worth further investigation. One approach to solving it is to find the number of blocks at each "level," then add them to find the total number of blocks. But here's another idea: could we first find the total number of blocks at one end, then multiply by the width of the step? That is, instead of thinking $(1 \times 4) + (2 \times 4) + (3 \times 4) + (4 \times 4) = 40$, could we think $(1 + 2 + 3 + 4) \times 4 = 40$?

Ask the students to make models of other figures where the total number of blocks is the product of the number of blocks in the base and the number of blocks in the figure's height. (Each column of blocks in the figure must be the same height for this to be true.) This is a demonstration of the formula volume (V) equals area of the base (B) times the height (h), which is how we can find the volume of any polygonal prism.

You may want to clarify that the base need not be on the bottom of the figure. The base can be any face that contains the same configuration of blocks as *every other* level of blocks. For example, in problems 1–3 on the worksheet, any face could be a base. In problem 4, the two faces (sides) containing 13 blocks could be a base. In problem 5, only the *ends* of the stair-steps could be bases. In problem 6, there is *no* base.

Numbers that read the same forwards and backwards are called *palindromes* or *palindromic numbers*. Some examples are shown below.

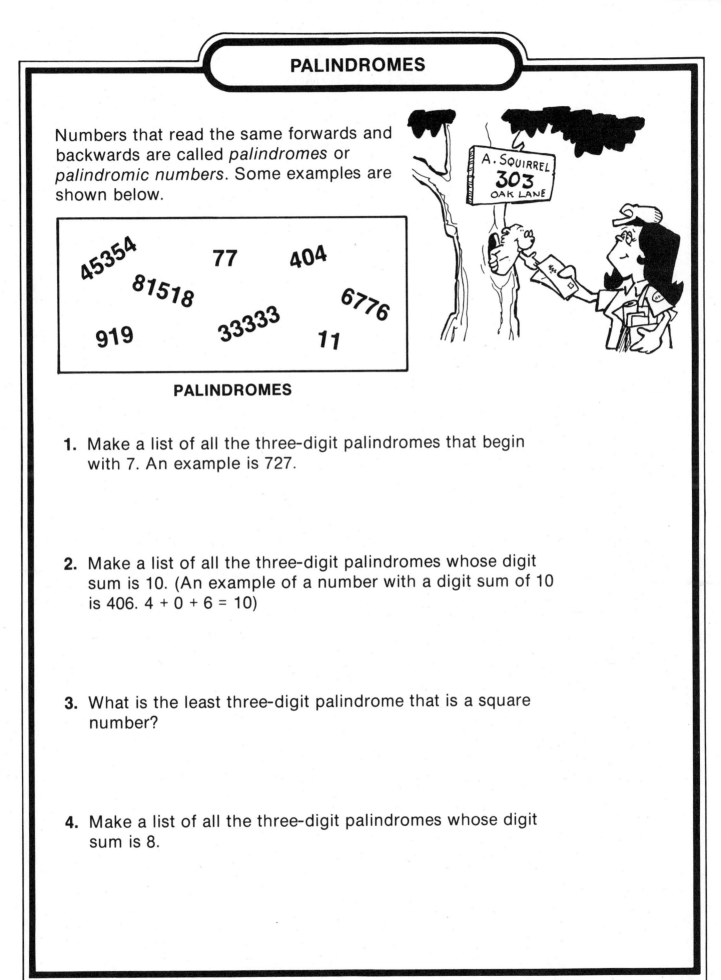

45354   77   404
81518   6776
919   33333
              11

PALINDROMES

1. Make a list of all the three-digit palindromes that begin with 7. An example is 727.

2. Make a list of all the three-digit palindromes whose digit sum is 10. (An example of a number with a digit sum of 10 is 406. 4 + 0 + 6 = 10)

3. What is the least three-digit palindrome that is a square number?

4. Make a list of all the three-digit palindromes whose digit sum is 8.

WARM-UP FOR PROBLEM 2

Discussion for
PALINDROMES

Answers

1. 707, 717, 727, 737, 747, 757, 767, 777, 787, 797
2. 181, 262, 343, 424, 505
3. 121 (11 × 11 = 121)
4. 161, 242, 323, 404

About the Problems

The purpose here is to reinforce place-value concepts and properties of numbers. Palindromes are just a motivational vehicle for the problems. Some students may ask if a number such as 040 is a three-digit number. The answer is no. The left-most digit must be a non-zero digit.

Emphasize to students that making a list with some system to it may help them insure that they do not overlook any numbers belonging on the list.

Getting Started

The examples given should offer enough help to get students started. You might have students ask themselves, "What would the *least* answer to the problem be?" This will help them generate answers in a sequential and complete list.

Solutions

1. If each three-digit palindrome begins with 7, it must also end with 7; thus only the tens digit can change. We can easily make a sequential list, then, beginning with the least digit (0) in the tens place and going up to the greatest digit (9): 707, 717, 727, 737, . . . 797.
2. Again, we know that the digits in the hundreds place and the units place must always be identical. We can begin by listing three-digit numbers with a blank in the tens place: 1_1, 2_2, 3_3, 4_4, 5_5. We stop at 5_5 because any number beyond that would exceed the digit sum of 10. It is then an easy matter to fill in the tens digit, which must always be the difference between 10 and the sum of the first and last digits.
3. Students may arrive at this answer by trial and error. The least possible three-digit square number is 100 (10 × 10), but 100 is not a palindrome. The *next* least square number is 11 × 11, or 121. That *is* a palindrome, so 121 must be the answer.
4. The system for solving this problem would be the same as for problem 2 (above).

Going Beyond

Have students create their own palindromic problems and solutions, then put together a set of problems for the entire class using the best student problems.

To get them started, give an example like this: "What is the greatest odd, three-digit palindrome that is divisible by 5?"

Problems like these help students to relate, compare, and sort number properties. They also develop good thinking skills, useful in many problem-solving situations.

PALINDROMETER

An odometer measures the distance a vehicle travels. The odometer here shows a palindromic number. What will be the next palindromic number to appear on the odometer?

PROBLEM 2

9

Discussion for
PALINDROMETER

Answer 36063

About the Problem

As was the case with the warm-up problem, the purpose here is to test an understanding of place value and number properties. The context of the problem requires students to think about what happens to numbers in different place-value positions as a number increases.

Getting Started

Most students at this level are reluctant to explore a problem because they don't think of math as a subject where exploration is expected or accepted. We need to change their attitudes on this point. For that reason, students should be left to play with this problem on their own, without any help, unless the problem itself needs to be clarified.

Solution

We can see that placing any number larger than 3 in the units position will require that we change the first digit on the left to the same number. That would make the entire number larger by at least 10,000. So, we may conclude that it is best to keep the 3 at each end for a minimum change in the number. The 5's cannot remain as they are, because when the 9 increases by 1, the 5 in the thousands place changes to a 6. The smallest center number, after the 5 in the thousands place changes to 6, is 0. To be palindromic, the digit in the tens place must also be 6. The resulting number is 36063. As you can see, this becomes a form of logic problem.

Going Beyond

Often students faced with a new kind of problem *finally* understand it only after the solution and the techniques for solving the problem have been discussed in some detail. At this point, the students are ready to test their understanding and practice their newly learned skills. Give them the chance to do so by extending the same problem. Ask them to find what the *next* two palindromic readings will be (beyond the answer you have already discussed).

DIGIT DISCOVERIES

Find the greatest three-digit number that is:

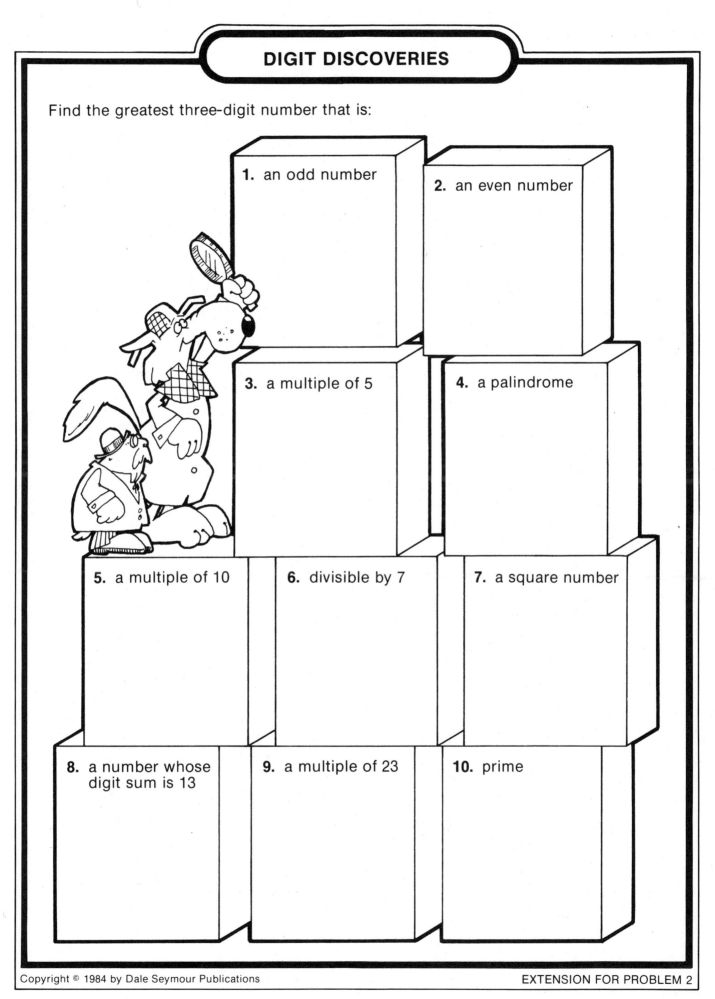

1. an odd number

2. an even number

3. a multiple of 5

4. a palindrome

5. a multiple of 10

6. divisible by 7

7. a square number

8. a number whose digit sum is 13

9. a multiple of 23

10. prime

EXTENSION FOR PROBLEM 2

DIGIT DISCOVERIES

Answers

1.	999	6.	994
2.	998	7.	961
3.	995	8.	940
4.	999	9.	989
5.	990	10.	997

About the Problems

This set of ten problems is arranged by general order of difficulty. The first few problems should be fairly easy; the last few may require quite a bit of investigation on the student's part.

Getting Started

Have the students look over all ten terms before they begin to be sure they know them and understand what is being asked for.

Solutions

Students should approach each problem by first considering the greatest possible three-digit number, 999. If 999 does not meet the requirements of the number they are looking for, then they should work backwards down through the 990's.

1. 999 fits the requirements.
2. 999 is odd; 998 is even.
3. If students know the test for divisibility by 5 (last digit is 5 or 0), they can jump immediately from 999 to 995, the largest number that ends in 5.
4. 999 fits the requirements.
5. If students know the test for divisibility by 10 (last digit is 0), they can jump immediately from 999 to 990, the largest number that meets that requirement.
6. The student can first try dividing 999 by 7. The quotient is 142 with a remainder of 5. In order to get an answer with *no* remainder, the dividend must then be 5 less than 999, or 994. A check shows that 994 is evenly divisible by 7. (Students who don't know the tests for divisibility by 5 and 10 could use the same approach on problems 3 and 5; this approach is also useful for problem 9.)

7. Most students will find the largest three-digit square by trial and error. For example, they might start with $30 \times 30 = 900$, then work up: $31 \times 31 = 961$, $32 \times 32 = 1024$—but that is a four-digit number, so the largest three-digit square must be 961.
8. Since we want the greatest three-digit number, we place a 9 in the hundreds place. The sum of the other two digits must be 4, so we place 4 in the tens place and 0 in the units place. 940 is the greatest number with a digit sum of 13.
9. We can use the same approach here as suggested for problem 6; we try dividing 999 by 23 and get a remainder of 10, so we try a dividend 10 less than 999, or 989, and find that it divides evenly by 23.
10. Problem 10 will be hard for most students. Working backwards, we know 999 is divisible by 9; 998 is divisible by 2; 997 is a candidate . . . Students may give 997 as the answer without knowing that they need to find out if 997 is divisible by primes less than 32 (the nearest square root). The student *should* check to see if 997 is divisible by 2, 3, 5, 7, 11, 13, 17, 19, 23, 29, and 31—a good time to have a calculator handy.

Going Beyond

An easy but effective extension of this worksheet is to change the word *greatest* to *least*. Here are the answers to the least three-digit number that is:

1. an odd number—101
2. an even number—100
3. a multiple of 5—100
4. a palindrome—101
5. a multiple of 10—100
6. divisible by 7—105
7. a square number—100
8. a number whose digit sum is 13—139
9. a multiple of 23—115
10. prime—101

Flo, Kit, Denise, Geri, and Lori are each in different rooms. No one is in a room that starts with the same first letter as her name. Lori is using the sink. Flo is setting the table. Geri is in a room next to Lori and Kit. Who is in each room? (Use the letters F, K, D, G, and L to eliminate possibilities.)

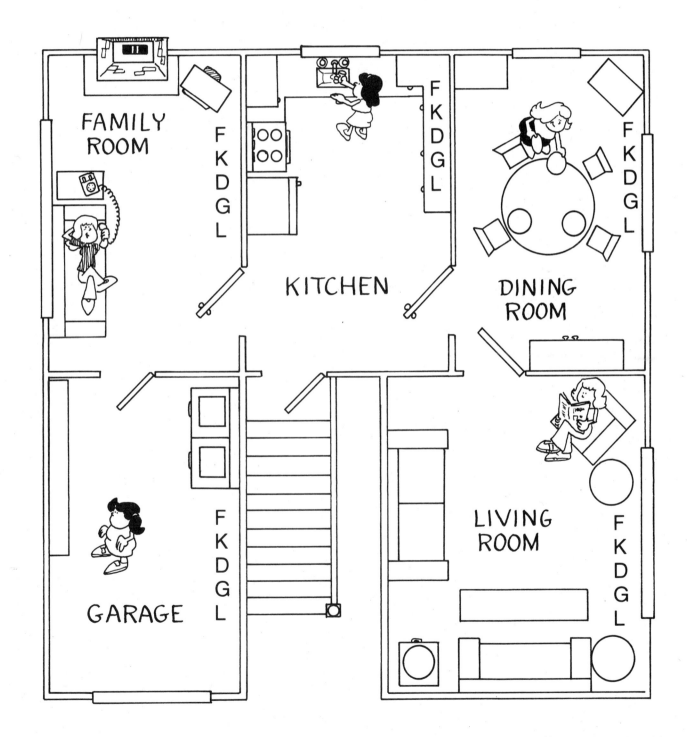

FAMILY ROOM

F K D G L

F K D G L

F K D G L

KITCHEN

DINING ROOM

F K D G L

GARAGE

F K D G L

LIVING ROOM

F K D G L

WARM-UP FOR PROBLEM 3

Discussion for
WHO'S WHERE?

Answers   Family room—Geri
Kitchen—Lori
Dining room—Flo
Garage—Kit
Living room—Denise

About the Problem

Using deductive logic is one important problem-solving strategy. This is a relatively simple logic problem, in which students read a series of clues and deduce the facts by putting the clues together.

If students have not solved this type of problem before, it may be a good idea to let them work together on the problem as a class.

Getting Started

Explain how students can use the diagram on the worksheet as an organizational chart. The letters in each room stand for the names of the five people. Students read through the clues and eliminate possibilities one at a time, crossing out a letter when it is known that the person is *not* in that room, and circling a letter when the person *is* found to be in that room.

Stress that students will need to read *each* of the clues, and then read through them once or twice more.

Many students will be accustomed to eating at a table in the kitchen, family room, or living room, so be sure they understand the significance of the *dining room* in this problem.

Solution

Since no one is in a room that starts with the same letter as her name, we can cross off Flo in the family room, Kit in the kitchen, Geri in the garage, and so forth.

Lori is using the sink, so she must be in the kitchen. We can circle L in the kitchen and cross out L in each of the other rooms.

Flo is setting the table, so she must be in the dining room.

Since Geri is in a room next to Lori and Kit, and one room next to Lori is already taken by Flo, Geri must be in the other room next to Lori, or the family room.

Geri is in a room next to Kit, so Kit must be in the garage. That leaves only Denise to be located in the living room.

Going Beyond

The best extension of a logic problem is *more* logic problems. Have the students proceed to the next two problems, *Jersey Jumble* and *Track Facts*.

JERSEY JUMBLE

Can you identify these players?

1. Abe wears a number divisible by 8.
2. Bob wears an odd number.
3. Cal likes rock music.
4. Dom is standing next to Abe.
5. Abe is shorter than Dom.
6. Bob is taller than Dom.
7. Cal is shorter than anyone.

PROBLEM 3

Discussion for
JERSEY JUMBLE

Answers   Abe wears number 88.
Bob wears number 11.
Cal wears number 32.
Dom wears number 25.

About the Problem

This kind of logic problem requires systematic organization. If students haven't done a problem of this type before, you might want to go through the previous problem, *Who's Where?*, as a class exercise.

Getting Started

The traditional way to solve logic problems is with a chart that shows all possibilities. If students need help, suggest that they design such a chart. Then possibilities can be marked off as they are eliminated. In fact, having students design an organizational chart of their own (like the one shown below) is a valuable exercise in itself.

	32	11	25	88
Abe				
Bob				
Cal				
Dom				

There are other ways to solve a problem like this, though, and you might want to give students the chance to play around and discover their own methods. One alternative system is described below under *Solution*.

Solution

Using the chart: Statement 1 tells us that Abe is wearing either number 32 or number 88, so we can write *no* for Abe under numbers 11 and 25. Statement 2 tells us that Bob's number is 11 or 25, so we write *no* for Bob under numbers 32 and 88. Statement 3 is not helpful. Statement 4 tells us that Dom's number is either 11 or 25, because Abe's is either 32 or 88. We write *no* for Dom under numbers 32 and 88.

Statement 5 doesn't help, since players 32 and 88 (Abe's possible numbers) are both shorter than players 11 and 25. Statement 6 gives us our first *yes* answers. We know that Bob and Dom are the two in the middle. Bob is taller, so Bob's number must be 11 and Dom's 25. We write *yes* on the chart to identify

them. Statement 7 identifies Cal's number as 32; therefore, Abe's must be 88.

	32	11	25	88
Abe	no	no	no	yes
Bob	no	yes	no	no
Cal	yes	no	no	no
Dom	no	no	yes	no

In an alternative approach, a student might use the pictures of the four players as the basis for organizing the facts, writing the names of the players under the appropriate pictures as the facts are learned.

That is: from the clues, Abe is either player 32 or player 88, so we write *Abe* under each of those figures. Bob is either player 11 or player 25, so we write *Bob* under them; likewise with Dom. When we learn Bob is taller than Dom, we know Bob must be player 11, so we circle his name there and cross it out under player 25; also cross out *Dom* under player 11 and circle it for player 25. We learn that Cal must be player 32, so we write and circle *Cal* under that figure, crossing out *Abe*, which means Abe must be player 88.

Going Beyond

The next order of difficulty is a logic problem with more layers of facts, involving a more complex organizational chart. The extension problem *Track Facts* is one of these.

TRACK FACTS

Identify each of these four track stars and their events. Their names are Mary, Sherrie, Teri, and Carey.

1. Sherrie is the sprinter.
2. The high jumper is not standing next to the sprinter.
3. The long jumper wears the largest number.
4. Carey is best friends with the distance runner.
5. Sherrie's number is 21.
6. The track coach is shorter than the sprinter.
7. Teri is standing between Carey and Sherrie.

Name _____   Name _____   Name _____   Name _____

Event _____   Event _____   Event _____   Event _____

EXTENSION FOR PROBLEM 3

Discussion for

TRACK FACTS

Answers   number 24, Carey, high jumper
number 27, Teri, long jumper
number 21, Sherrie, sprinter
number 26, Mary, distance runner

About the Problem

Like all logic problems, this one will require some careful organization on the part of the students. They need to determine which information is relevant and how to relate each piece of information to other data in the problem.

Getting Started

Students who found the chart for *Jersey Jumble* helpful may want to set up a chart like the one used in the solution below. Then, as they read each statement, they can mark the chart with any information that would identify or eliminate a possibility. Remind students that with this type of problem, they may need to read through the statements *two or three times* before they discover all the information needed to solve the problem.

As with *Jersey Jumble*, a student might prefer to use the pictures as a basis for organizing facts, rather than the chart. Allow students the freedom to solve the problem by whatever system feels most comfortable to them.

Solution

Statement 1 identifies Sherrie as the sprinter, so all others can be eliminated from the sprinter column. Statement 2 is not helpful at this point. (It will be helpful later, when more facts are known.) Statement 3 identifies the long jumper as number 27, which tells us that Sherrie (the sprinter) is not number 27. Statement 4 tells us that Carey is not the distance runner. Statement 5 tells us that Sherrie's number is 21. Statement 6 is irrelevant. Statement 7 tells us that Teri is standing between Carey and Sherrie (who is number 21), so Teri has to be wear-

ing number 27, and Carey must be wearing number 24. This leaves only number 26 for Mary, since the numbers of all the others have been identified.

Now we start back through the facts a second time. Statement 2 tells us that the high jumper is *not* number 26 or number 27, the two who are standing next to the sprinter (number 21); thus the high jumper must be wearing number 24. Since we know that Carey is wearing number 24, we know that Carey is the high jumper. Statement 3 identifies the long jumper as number 27. Teri's number is 27, so Teri is the long jumper. Mary must then be the distance runner, as the other three have been identified.

A student who uses the pictures for organizing the facts might proceed as follows:

None of the clues are immediately useful until statement 3, when we can write *long jumper* under the girl wearing 27. Statement 4 tells us nothing yet, but with statement 5 we can write *Sherrie* under the girl wearing 21. Statement 7 then lets us write *Teri* under the girl wearing 27 and *Carey* under the girl wearing 24, and therefore *Mary* (the only one left) under the girl wearing 26.

Going back through the clues: from statement 1, we can write *sprinter* under number 21 (Sherrie). From statement 2, we write *high jumper* under number 24 (Carey). That leaves only *distance runner* to be written under number 26 (Mary)—and the problem is solved.

Going Beyond

Two excellent sources for more logic problems of varying degrees of difficulty are the books *Quizzles* and *More Quizzles* by Wayne Williams. The student-worksheet versions of these books are available in reproducible blackline-master form from Dale Seymour Publications:

Quizzles (1982), order number DS01285
More Quizzles (1984), order number DS01469

	sprinter	high jumper	long jumper	distance runner	21	24	26	27
Mary	no	no	no	yes	no	no	yes	no
Sherrie	yes	no	no	no	yes	no	no	no
Teri	no	no	yes	no	no	no	no	yes
Carey	no	yes	no	no	no	yes	no	no

1. How many days are there in one million seconds?

2. The life expectancy of an average person living in the United States, Canada, or Australia is approximately 74 years. Assuming you will live exactly this long, how many hours do you have left to live?

WARM-UP FOR PROBLEM 4

Answers

1. about 11½ days (11.574)
2. 648,240 hours *minus* the number of hours the student has lived to date. Or, if you take leap years into account, 648,684 hours minus the number of hours the student has already lived. (For approximate answers, see *Solutions* below.)

About the Problems

Students are usually fascinated by very large numbers. These problems let them think about the steps involved in converting large units of time into smaller units of time, and vice versa.

Getting Started

On the second problem, you may need to clarify whether you want to consider leap years or not. The problem is much simpler if students simply figure 365 days per year rather than 365¼ (or 365.25).

Also, some students may be concerned that they do not know exactly what hour they were born. That level of accuracy is not important here. Help students understand that when we work with large numbers, we often deal with estimates and approximate numbers, and they should be comfortable with calculating *approximately* how long they have lived.

Solutions

1. This problem might be approached by finding how many minutes are in one million seconds, then converting the minutes to hours and the hours to days, as follows:
   a. 1,000,000 seconds = $16,666.\overline{6}$ minutes
      $(1,000,000 \div 60)$
   b. $16,666.\overline{6}$ minutes = $277.\overline{7}$ hours
      $(16,666.\overline{6} \div 60)$
   c. $277.\overline{7}$ hours = 11.574074 days (about 11½ days)
      $(277.\overline{7} \div 24)$

   Alternatively, a student might first find the number of seconds there are in one day:
      60 seconds/minute × 60 minutes/hour ×
      24 hours = 86,400 seconds
   Then, dividing 1,000,000 seconds by 86,400 seconds gives us 11.57074, or about 11½ days.

2. *Solution ignoring leap years:*
   First we find how many hours there are in 74 years (find how many days, then convert days to hours).
   a. 74 years = 27,010 days
      (74 × 365)
   b. 27,010 days = 648,240 hours
      (27,010 × 24)

   Students then figure about how many hours they have already lived. For example, a student 11 years and 3 months old would find:
      11 years + 3 months = 4015 days + 91 days
      4015 + 91 = 4106 days
      4106 × 24 = 98,544 hours
   Subtracting that from the total hours in 74 years:
      648,240 – 98,544 = 549,696
   The student thus has about 549,696 hours left in his or her lifetime.

   Solution including leap years:
   First we find the number of hours in 74 years, using 365.25 as the number of days per year.
   a. 74 × 365.25 = 27,028.5 days
   b. 27,028.5 × 24 = 648,684 hours

   Students then calculate about how many hours they have already lived, following the steps above but figuring 365.25 days in a year.

   Approximate answers (ignoring leap years):
   For 10-year-olds: 648,240 – 87,600 = 560,640 hours
   For 11-year-olds: 648,240 – 96,360 = 551,880 hours
   For 12-year-olds: 648,240 – 105,120 = 543,120 hours
   For 13-year-olds: 648,240 – 113,880 = 534,360 hours

Going Beyond

For more work with large numbers, give the students the following two problems, *How Big Is a Million?* and *Number Names.*

Estimate, investigate, then calculate:

1. How long would one million dollars be, laid out end to end?
2. How high would a stack of one million one-cent coins be?

PROBLEM 4

HOW BIG IS A MILLION?

Answers

1. *Using U.S. dollars:*

15,500,000 cm	6,125,000 inches
155,000 m	510,417 feet
155 km	97 miles

   Using Canadian dollars:

15,300,000 cm
153,000 m
153 km

   Using Australian dollars:

13,800,000 cm
138,000 m
138 km

2. United States, Canadian, and Australian one-cent coins are all approximately the same thickness. Using any of them:

142,857 cm	55,555 inches
1,429 m	4,630 feet
1.43 km	9/10 mile

About the Problems

Most students seem to have a strong interest in the question, "How big is a million?" These problems give students an opportunity to test their estimation, research, and computational skills. Since measures are approximate, answers may vary somewhat, especially because they are multiplied by one million. The important ideas here are as follows:

1. to get a general feeling for the size of one million.
2. to choose the proper operations for solving the problem.
3. to compute the researched numbers with accuracy.

Getting Started

To measure the thickness of one cent, it helps to have a micrometer available. If this is not possible, students should realize that they will get a more accurate figure if they measure an entire roll of coins and find an average thickness. Obviously, some older coins may be worn down some. Stress that in these problems, minute precision is not important.

Solutions

These problems simply involve finding the width of the dollar or thickness of the coin, then multiplying by one million. Obtaining the answer in both English and metric units points out the obvious advantages of the metric system.

The measures to work with are as follows:

- One United States dollar measures approximately 15.5 centimeters or 6⅛ inches.
- One Canadian dollar measures approximately 15.3 centimeters.
- One Australian dollar measures approximately 13.8 centimeters.
- Seven one-cent coins stacked together measure about 1 cm. Eighteen such coins stacked measure about 1 inch. Dividing 1 by 7 (if using metric units) or 1 by 18 (if using English units) gives us the number we need to multiply by one million.

Going Beyond

In a class discussion, ask students how many dollars end-to-end would be required to stretch across the country.

Select a number of items, large and small, and ask students to estimate the size, weight, or cost of *one million* of each item. Then have the students research and calculate to find a more accurate answer. Practice like this helps improve estimation skills.

NUMBER NAMES

Names of our decimal numeration system are shown below.

DUODECILLIONS	UNDECILLIONS	DECILLIONS	NONILLIONS	OCTILLIONS	SEPTILLIONS	SEXTILLIONS	QUINTILLIONS	QUADRILLIONS	TRILLIONS	BILLIONS	MILLIONS	THOUSANDS	UNITS
hundreds tens units	hundreds tens units	hundreds tens units	hundreds tens units	hundreds tens units	hundreds tens units	hundreds tens units	hundreds tens units	hundreds tens units	hundreds tens units	hundreds tens units	hundreds tens units	hundreds tens units	hundreds tens units

Write in numerals:

1. One billion, five hundred seventeen million

_____

2. One hundred thirty-three sextillion

_____

3. Nine quintillion, six hundred seventy-two trillion, fifteen

_____

4. Sixty-three duodecillion

_____

Write in words:

5. 800,000,000,000,000,000,000,000,000

_____

6. 56,000,056,000,056,000,056

_____

7. 9,000,000,000,009

_____

8. 1,234,567,890,123,456

_____

_____

_____

EXTENSION FOR PROBLEM 4

NUMBER NAMES

Answers

1. 1,517,000,000
2. 133,000,000,000,000,000,000,000
3. 9,000,672,000,000,000,015
4. 63,000,000,000,000,000,000,000,000,000,000,000,000,000 (63 followed by 39 zeros)
5. Eight hundred sextillion
6. Fifty-six quintillion, fifty-six trillion, fifty-six million, fifty-six
7. Nine trillion, nine
8. One quadrillion, two hundred thirty-four trillion, five hundred sixty-seven billion, eight hundred ninety million, one hundred twenty-three thousand, four hundred fifty-six

About the Problems

Most students are curious about the larger number names and, consequently, are motivated to explore them. Although these names are rarely used, it is valuable for students to know that place names have historically been assigned to very large numbers. These problems provide an opportunity to review some important rules in writing numbers in word and numeral form.

Getting Started

Remind students that they should *not* use the word *and* in reading or writing whole numbers (*and* is reserved for the decimal point position; 2.3 is read two *and* three tenths). When writing out numbers in words, we use commas between each nonzero major division that we name. Nonzero two-digit numbers greater than 20 are hyphenated to eliminate ambiguities.

Beyond these rules, the chart should provide sufficient help to get the students started.

Solutions

Refer to the answers. If student answers differ, take some time to explore why their answers are wrong and explain what their answers represent.

Going Beyond

If students are interested in additional place-value positions, those that come after duodecillions are as follows: tredecillions, quattuordecillion, quindecillion, sexdecillion, septendecillion, octodecillion, novemdecillion, vigintillion. You may want to mention that 10^{100} is a googol.

This is a logical time to discuss expanded notation and scientific notation, where very large numbers are expressed as a decimal number between 1 and 10 multiplied by a power of 10. For example, nine trillion is written 9×10^{12}. Students who have just experienced the inconvenience of writing thirty-nine zeroes (for problem 4, 63 duodecillion) will appreciate the usefulness of scientific notation.

RECTANGLE SEARCH

Count *all* the rectangles in each figure.

1.

2.

3.

Remember, a square is a rectangle!

4.

5.

6.

7.

WARM-UP FOR PROBLEM 5

Discussion for

RECTANGLE SEARCH

Answers: 1. 3   5. 17
            2. 6   6. 15
            3. 11   7. 36
            4. 11

About the Problems

These problems present a need for some organized listing. They test the student's visual perception and may require some awareness of patterns.

Getting Started

Suggest that students organize their counting by looking for *types* of rectangles.

Students may find it helpful to mark dots and lines on the figures as they count them, as shown in the example below:

3 one-block rectangles
2 two-block rectangles
1 three-block rectangle

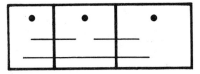

3 + 2 + 1 = 6

If necessary, clarify that a square is a special rectangle; therefore all squares should be counted.

Solutions

As soon as students see that some rectangles are formed by two or more smaller rectangles, they may think of counting all single blocks first, then rectangles formed by two smaller blocks, three smaller blocks, and so forth.

1. 2 (ones) + 1 (two) = 3 rectangles
2. 3 (ones) + 2 (twos) + 1 (three) = 6 rectangles
3. 5 (ones) + 4 (twos) + 2 (threes) = 11 rectangles
4. 5 (ones) + 2 (twos) + 1 (three) + 2 (fours) + 1 (five) = 11 rectangles
5. 7 (ones) + 6 (twos) + 3 (threes) + 1 (four) = 17 rectangles
6. 6 (ones) + 6 (twos) + 2 (threes) + 1 (four) = 15 rectangles
7. 12 (ones) + 11 (twos) + 7 (threes) + 4 (fours) + 2 (fives) = 36 rectangles

Going Beyond

Students may be interested in designing their own problems of this type. If they design a problem, they should also solve it. Students will enjoy trading their problems or turning them in so that you can select an interesting set for the entire class to solve. You may need to establish some guidelines in order to keep the problems from becoming too complex or difficult. For example: Limit the number of rectangles to 50.

Checkerboard Squares will be a nice extension to these problems.

How many different squares of all sizes are on a checkerboard? Hints: Organize your listing. Look for patterns!

PROBLEM 5

Discussion for
CHECKERBOARD SQUARES

Answer   204 squares

About the Problem

This kind of problem will make clear to students the need for an organizational plan. There are enough different-sized squares that students will need to create a list or a chart to keep track of the squares of different sizes.

Getting Started

It is helpful to label the different-sized squares in some manner so students can talk about them. Unit squares can be referred to as "one-by-ones" (1 × 1), the next size as "two-by-twos," and so forth.

Students should approach this problem by making an organized list. Watching the ways different students create such a list can give you insights into their organizational skills. Only a sequential list will help them see the patterns involved.

Some students may have trouble visualizing the overlapping positions of various-sized squares. It may help them to trace the position of the square with a finger. For a more concrete approach, give students graph paper and have them outline separate 8-by-8 grids. They can then mark or trace squares of each size on the different grids.

Solution

There are 64 small one-by-one squares (8 × 8). There are seven two-by-twos in each double row, and there are seven double rows. This gives 49 (7 × 7) two-by-twos. We can proceed in this same way to count three-by-threes, four-by-fours, and so on.

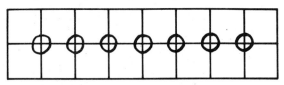

A complete list of the squares of all sizes is given below. Your better students, if they have done anything with square numbers, will likely notice the pattern of consecutive square numbers.

SIZE OF SQUARE	SQUARES IN ROW		SQUARES IN COLUMN	TOTAL SQUARES
one-by-one	8	×	8	64
two-by-two	7	×	7	49
three-by-three	6	×	6	36
four-by-four	5	×	5	25
five-by-five	4	×	4	16
six-by-six	3	×	3	9
seven-by-seven	2	×	2	4
eight-by-eight	1	×	1	1

total 204

Going Beyond

For more practice with this type of problem, ask students to find the number of squares in a 3-by-5 grid, in a 4-by-7 grid, and so forth.

Patterns in a 3-by-5 grid

SIZE OF SQUARE	SQUARES IN ROW		SQUARES IN COLUMN	TOTAL SQUARES	PATTERN
one-by-one	5	×	3	15	5 × 3
two-by-two	4	×	2	8	(5–1) × (3–1)
three-by-three	3	×	1	3	(5–2) × (3–2)

total 26

Patterns in a 4-by-7 grid

SIZE OF SQUARE	SQUARES IN ROW		SQUARES IN COLUMN	TOTAL SQUARES	PATTERN
one-by-one	7	×	4	28	7 × 4
two-by-two	6	×	3	18	(7–1) × (4–1)
three-by-three	5	×	2	10	(7–2) × (4–2)
four-by-four	4	×	1	4	(7–3) × (4–3)

total 60

SETTING THE TABLE

Study the patterns in the tables below. Fill in the blanks with the numbers that continue the given pattern in each table.

1.

TERM	NO.	PATTERN
1st	1	1
2nd	2	1 + 1
3rd	3	1 + 1 + 1
4th	4	1 + 1 + 1 + 1
5th	5	1 + 1 + 1 + 1 + 1
⋮	⋮	⋮
10th	_____	1 + 1 + 1 + · · · + 1

2.

TERM	NO.	PATTERN
1st	1	1
2nd	3	1 + 2
3rd	6	1 + 2 + 3
4th	10	1 + 2 + 3 + 4
5th	_____	1 + 2 + 3 + 4 + 5
⋮	⋮	⋮
10th	_____	1 + 2 + 3 + · · · + 10

3.

TERM	NO.	PATTERN
1st	1	1 × 1
2nd	4	2 × 2
3rd	_____	3 × 3
4th	_____	_____
5th	_____	_____
⋮	⋮	⋮
10th	_____	_____

4.

TERM	NO.	PATTERN
1st	0	5 × 0
2nd	5	5 × 1
3rd	_____	5 × 2
4th	_____	_____
5th	_____	_____
6th	_____	_____
⋮	⋮	⋮
10th	_____	_____
⋮	⋮	⋮
100th	_____	_____

5.

TERM	NO.	PATTERN
1st	1	2 × 0 + 1
2nd	3	2 × 1 + 1
3rd	5	2 × 2 + 1
4th	_____	2 × _____
5th	_____	_____
6th	_____	_____
⋮	⋮	⋮
10th	_____	_____
⋮	⋮	⋮
100th	_____	_____

6.

TERM	NO.	PATTERN
1st	_____	1
2nd	_____	1 + 3
3rd	_____	1 + 3 + 5
4th	_____	1 + 3 + 5 + 7
5th	_____	_____
⋮	⋮	⋮
10th	_____	_____

(You can use three dots to abbreviate long patterns.)

7.

TERM	NO.	PATTERN
1st	1	1 × 1 × 1
2nd	_____	2 × 2 × 2
3rd	_____	3 × 3 × 3
4th	_____	_____
5th	_____	_____
⋮	⋮	⋮
10th	_____	_____
⋮	⋮	⋮
100th	_____	_____

8.

TERM	NO.	PATTERN
1st	1	1
2nd	_____	1 × 2
3rd	_____	1 × 2 × 3
4th	_____	1 × 2 × 3 × 4
5th	_____	_____
6th	_____	_____
⋮	⋮	⋮
10th	_____	1 × 2 × 3 × · · · × 10
11th	_____	_____

(You can use three dots to abbreviate long patterns.)

EXTENSION FOR PROBLEM 5

SETTING THE TABLE

Answers

1.

TERM	NO.	PATTERN
1st	1	1
2nd	2	1 + 1
3rd	3	1 + 1 + 1
4th	4	1 + 1 + 1 + 1
5th	5	1 + 1 + 1 + 1 + 1
⋮	⋮	⋮
10th	**10**	1 + 1 + 1 + · · · + 1

2.

TERM	NO.	PATTERN
1st	1	1
2nd	3	1 + 2
3rd	6	1 + 2 + 3
4th	10	1 + 2 + 3 + 4
5th	**15**	1 + 2 + 3 + 4 + 5
⋮	⋮	⋮
10th	**55**	1 + 2 + 3 + · · · + 10

3.

TERM	NO.	PATTERN
1st	1	1 × 1
2nd	4	2 × 2
3rd	**9**	3 × 3
4th	**16**	4 × 4
5th	**25**	5 × 5
⋮	⋮	⋮
10th	**100**	10 × 10

4.

TERM	NO.	PATTERN
1st	0	5 × 0
2nd	5	5 × 1
3rd	**10**	5 × 2
4th	**15**	5 × 3
5th	**20**	5 × 4
6th	**25**	5 × 5
⋮	⋮	⋮
10th	**45**	5 × 9
⋮	⋮	⋮
100th	**495**	5 × 99

5.

TERM	NO.	PATTERN
1st	1	2 × 0 + 1
2nd	3	2 × 1 + 1
3rd	5	2 × 2 + 1
4th	**7**	2 × **3** + 1
5th	**9**	2 × **4** + 1
6th	**11**	2 × **5** + 1
⋮	⋮	⋮
10th	**19**	2 × **9** + 1
⋮	⋮	⋮
100th	**199**	2 × **99** + 1

6.

TERM	NO.	PATTERN
1st	**1**	1
2nd	**4**	1 + 3
3rd	**9**	1 + 3 + 5
4th	**16**	1 + 3 + 5 + 7
5th	**25**	1 + 3 + 5 + 7 + 9
⋮	⋮	⋮
10th	**100**	1 + 3 + 5 + · · · + 19

(You can use three dots to abbreviate long patterns.)

7.

TERM	NO.	PATTERN
1st	1	1 × 1 × 1
2nd	**8**	2 × 2 × 2
3rd	**27**	3 × 3 × 3
4th	**64**	4 × 4 × 4
5th	**125**	5 × 5 × 5
⋮	⋮	⋮
10th	**1,000**	10 × 10 × 10
⋮	⋮	⋮
100th	**79,507**	43 × 43 × 43

8.

TERM	NO.	PATTERN
1st	1	1
2nd	**2**	1 × 2
3rd	**6**	1 × 2 × 3
4th	**24**	1 × 2 × 3 × 4
5th	**120**	1 × 2 × 3 × 4 × 5
6th	**720**	1 × 2 × 3 × 4 × 5 × 6
⋮	⋮	⋮
10th	**3,628,800**	1 × 2 × 3 × · · · × 10
11th	**39,916,800**	1 × 2 × 3 × · · · × 11

(You can use three dots to abbreviate long patterns.)

About the Problem

These problems are designed to (1) familiarize students with table formats, (2) make students pattern-conscious, and (3) show some alternate forms of basic number concepts, such as *odd numbers* and *square numbers*.

You may have to do considerable explaining and hand-holding if students have never seen this problem format before. However, give students the chance to decode these problems on their own before you begin class discussion.

Getting Started

The three-dot notation is used to indicate that the same pattern continues. It is simply a way to abbreviate what would otherwise be a lengthy notation. Students may want to use this notation themselves on problems 6 and 8.

Encourage students to skip around and do what they can. A calculator will be especially helpful on problems 7 and 8.

Solutions

See answers. If your students are just beginning to recognize patterns, most will not pick up any pattern in the sequence of numbers, but they should be able to extend the patterns given. Once the *pattern* is complete, the missing number can be determined by simple computation.

Going Beyond

During class discussion on these number patterns, help students identify the types of number patterns shown in the tables. They include:

1. counting numbers (natural numbers)
2. triangular numbers (can be arranged in a triangular array)
3. square numbers
4. multiples of five
5. odd numbers
6. square numbers
7. cubic numbers
8. factorials

	V	W	X	Y	Z
A	3	8	9	6	1
B	8	1	5	2	7
C	3	9	1	5	4
D	5	6	7	3	1
E	8	4	0	7	2

The answer is...

Use the grid to answer these questions.

1. Which row contains the greatest five-digit number?
What is the number?

2. Which row contains the greatest four-digit number?
What is the number?

3. Which column has the greatest digit sum?
What is the sum?

4. Which row has the least digit product?
What is the product?

5. Circle sets of three adjacent number blocks that add to 13.

Adjacent number blocks must share a common side.

How many sets can you find?

RIGHT

5	6
	2

7
1
5

WRONG (do not share a side)

	3
5	
5	

2
	4
	7

6. Which square of four digits could be used to
form the greatest four-digit number? Fill it in below.
What is the number?

Answers

1. Row *E*, 84,072
2. Row *C*, 9,154
3. Column *W*, digit sum of 28
4. Row *E*, digit product of zero
5. There are eight sets:

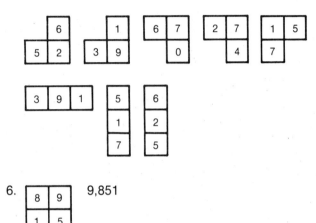

6. 9,851

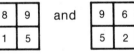

About the Problem

This format provides for a variety of questions that drill students on their understanding of computation or place-value concepts. It also gives students practice in spatial visualization and organization skills.

Getting Started

Since there are six straightforward questions here, getting into the problem should not be difficult for students.

You may need to clarify that in problems 1 through 4, students are not allowed to rearrange the positions of digits.

Solutions

1. We begin by looking for the greatest digit in the first position, which is 8 in rows *B* and *E*. We then look at the digits in the second position, and note that 4 (row *E*) is greater than 1 (row *B*), so the answer is row *E*: 84,072.

2. Since we are looking for a four-digit number, we know that the left-most digit must fall in either column *V* or column *W*. We look for the greatest digit in those columns: it is the 9 in row *C*. So the greatest four-digit number is 9,154 in row *C*.

3. To solve this, we simply add all the digits in each column. The sums are:

   column *V*—27
   column *W*—28
   column *X*—22
   column *Y*—23
   column *Z*—15

   So column *W* has the greatest digit sum, 28.

4. Our first thought is that we must multiply all the digits in each row. The alert student, however, will spot the 0 in row *E* and recognize that the product of that row must be 0, which would be the least digit product. This will save the trouble of multiplying all the other rows.

5. To insure that we find all the sets, we need to organize our search. We can start by identifying every acceptable configuration of number blocks:

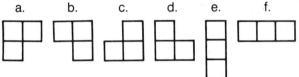

   Then, one at a time we can test each configuration, row by row and column by column, summing the digits in each position. This way we should find all eight sets shown in the answers.

6. We begin by locating the greatest single digits in the grid: the 9's in row *A* and row *C*. The 9 in row *A* can be part of only two four-digit squares:

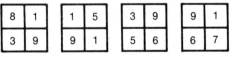

   The greatest number here can be made with the square on the left, or 9,851.

   Now we look at the 9 in row *C*, which can be part of four squares:

   Only the first of these has the digit 8 (with the potential to beat 9,851), but the greatest number to be made with this square is 9,831. That means the square above makes the greatest four-digit number: 9,851.

Going Beyond

Ask students to make up their own questions similar to the six on the worksheet. This will help prepare them for the next problem, *You're the Inventor*.

Make up some problems or puzzles using this grid.

	L	M	N	P	Q	R	S	T	U	W
A	3	6	0	2	8	4	9	0	6	1
B	1	5	4	7	1	9	2	5	3	8
C	8	3	5	8	0	6	9	2	4	2
D	4	0	2	5	4	9	3	6	8	0
E	9	1	6	9	3	9	5	0	9	4
F	8	4	3	0	9	1	7	7	1	6
G	2	6	5	2	8	5	2	4	5	8
H	0	3	7	4	3	7	6	3	0	9
J	5	1	2	7	0	1	7	7	2	1
K	3	7	6	1	8	7	4	8	5	6

PROBLEM 6

YOU'RE THE INVENTOR

Answers   Will vary. See samples below.

About the Problem

This problem was designed to get students involved. Creating math problems *themselves* helps reduce students' problem-solving fears. It also shows that imagination and creativity do have a place in mathematics.

Getting Started

The warm-up problem *Place-A-Value* may be a prerequisite for most students. Be sure that students know the meanings of the terms *row* (horizontal) and *column* (vertical), and that they use those terms in the problems they create.

Sample Problems and Ideas

1. For which rows is the digit product a nonzero number? (testing the multiplication property of zero)
2. Find a path of odd digits from one corner to the other. You may connect digits horizontally, vertically, or diagonally. (testing the concept of odd numbers)
3. Find the longest string of adjacent odd digits.
4. In which row do you find the largest 2-digit number? 3-digit? 5-digit? (testing place value)
5. Mark all *pairs* of adjacent digits, horizontal, vertical, or diagonal, whose products are 24.
6. Mark all pairs of adjacent digits whose sum is 10.
7. How many squares of four digits can you find that have equal *corner sums* (the sums of the digits in opposite corners)?

   Example:
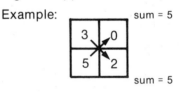

8. How many squares of four digits can you find in which one *corner sum* equals the other *corner product*?

   Example:
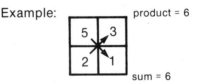

9. If you could pick five digits from any row, without rearranging the digits, which row would give you the greatest 5-digit number? The least? (The first digit cannot be zero.)
10. Can you find a digit chain that gives your phone number? Your birthday month, day, and year? You may move horizontally, vertically, or diagonally.

Going Beyond

Students can have a problem exchange and try solving each other's creations.

Use the following information in story problems that *you* create. Make your problems interesting and challenging. Give solutions to your problems. You can add facts and figures of your own, but you *must* use the facts given below.

1. 13 coins
no coins worth one dollar

2. 50 meters of fencing
8 fence posts

3. 200 general admission tickets
100 reserved seats
reserved tickets cost $1.00 more

EXTENSION FOR PROBLEM 6

CREATE-A-PROBLEM

Answers Will vary. See samples below.

About the Problem

By occasionally designing problems of their own, students better understand the makeup of word problems. Once students see that a number of different kinds of problems can be made from the same basic information, they will begin to understand the need to read a problem *carefully*.

Many students will make up problems that are similar to textbook problems they are familiar with. You may want to put together a worksheet of several different student-created problems based on the same basic data.

Getting Started

You might want to suggest that students put extraneous information in their problems. Having done this themselves, they will be more aware of the need to look for relevant and irrelevant information when they solve problems in the future.

Sample Problems

1. a. Wilbert has $2.09 in his pocket. He has 13 coins and none of these is a dollar coin. Give one combination of coins he might have. (*eight 25¢ coins, one 5¢ coin, and four 1¢ coins*)

   b. How could you divide 13 coins between two people so they would each get the same amount? None of the 13 is a dollar coin. What coins and amounts would each get? (*Answers will vary. One possible combination is to give one person two 25¢ coins and three 5¢ coins, or 65¢, and the other person five 10¢ coins and three 5¢ coins, or 65¢.*)

   c. Jolene gave the clerk a dollar for a 36¢ item. What were the 13 coins she got back in change? (*one 25¢ coin, three 10¢ coins, and nine 1¢ coins*)

2. a. Fencing costs $3.00 per meter. Posts cost $6.00 each. If Jake buys 50 meters of fencing and 8 posts, how much does he pay for the material? (*$198*)

   b. If 8 fence posts are needed for every 50 meters of fencing, how many posts would be needed for 300 meters of fencing? (*48 posts*)

   c. 50 meters of fencing is arranged in a square. If 8 posts are evenly spaced along the fence, how far apart are the posts? (*6.25 m*)

3. a. Central auditorium has 300 seats. The committee decides to reserve 100 seats in the front and charge one dollar more for reserved seats than for general admission. If general admission seats sell for $1.50, how much money could be made if all the tickets were sold? (*$550*)

   b. The school band is selling 100 reserved seat tickets and 200 general admission seat tickets. Reserved tickets are $1 more than general admission. What does the band need to charge for general admission to earn at least $500 if they sell all the tickets? (*$1.25*)

   c. We sold two hundred general admission tickets to the basketball game for $2.75 each. Reserved tickets cost $1 more than general admission. We sold half as many reserved tickets as we did general admission tickets. How much money did we take in on reserved seat sales? (*$375*)

Going Beyond

Challenge students to create more story problems for a Best Problem Contest. You may want to provide guidelines as to the math concepts to be covered, the difficulty level, the number of steps involved in solution, and so forth. Contest entrants should submit their problems with solutions on a separate page. You might allow students to judge the problems, preferably without the names of the creators attached. Such an exercise will help students think about the formulation of a problem and give them more confidence in attacking problems themselves.

RECTANGLE RIDDLE

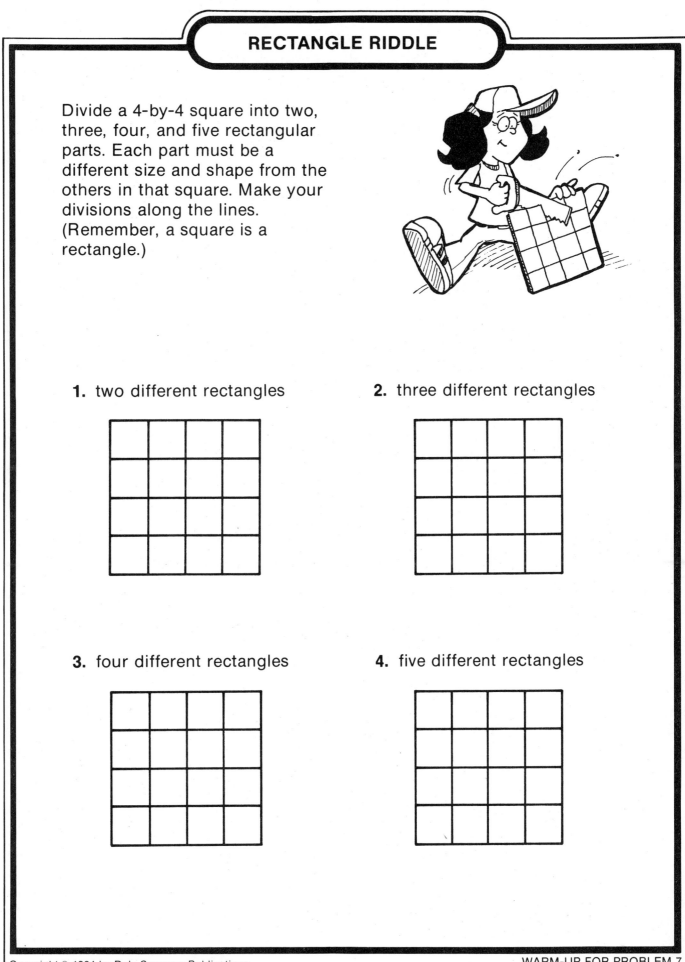

Divide a 4-by-4 square into two, three, four, and five rectangular parts. Each part must be a different size and shape from the others in that square. Make your divisions along the lines. (Remember, a square is a rectangle.)

1. two different rectangles

2. three different rectangles

3. four different rectangles

4. five different rectangles

Discussion for
RECTANGLE RIDDLE

Answers

1.

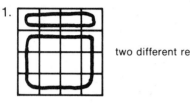

two different rectangles

2.

 OR OR

three different rectangles

3.

OR

four different rectangles

4.

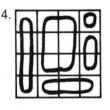

five different rectangles

About the Problem

This problem will exercise students' visual perception skills.

Getting Started

Be sure students understand that none of the parts of any one square can be the same size or shape.

Students can begin by using a pencil and eraser in trial-and-error techniques, making sketches on the grids given on the worksheet. Handing out graph paper, if available, might be helpful for students seeking additional solutions.

Solutions

Students might take an organized approach, thinking: "Can I use a one-unit rectangle? A two-unit rectangle? A three-unit rectangle?" and so forth.

Going Beyond

Ask students if their answers are the only ones possible. (An answer is considered the same as another if the parts are the same sizes, regardless of their orientation in the grid.)

Have students try the same exercise with 5-by-5 squares.

On a 5-by-5 grid, show how these puzzle pieces can form a square.

Answer

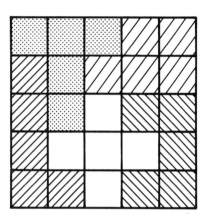

About the Problem

This problem will test the students' abilities to make a transposition from three dimensions to two dimensions. It will also require them to invent a procedure to explore solutions, as well as a means of *presenting* their solution.

Getting Started

Part of the value of this problem is letting the students go through the preliminary thinking process: deciding how they should approach a solution, and how they will graphically or physically present the solution.

It is best not to suggest specific approaches to the problem unless the students have already thought about it for some time and are still at a loss for an approach.

Solution

Some students may wish to create block models from wooden cubes. Others may explore possible solutions with graph paper, either by drawing or by cutting out the puzzle shapes.

Sometimes, with a bit of luck, the solution will come quickly and easily. For others, the problem may be quite challenging.

Students who make a model by cutting up graph paper into appropriate shapes may find that they need to color the right side of each piece to avoid flopping any shapes as they manipulate them. Students following this strategy may also want to keep a 5-by-5 base grid (as a reminder of the outside limits) under the puzzle pieces they are moving around.

Going Beyond

Tangram puzzles can provide students with additional activities similar to this problem. Tangram activities are available that are appropriate for students with a wide range of perceptual aptitudes. The products below include puzzles suitable for people from grade K to adult.

Tangramath by Dale Seymour. Palo Alto, Calif.: Creative Publications, 1971.
Perceptual Puzzle Blocks by Dale and Margo Seymour. Palo Alto, Calif.: Creative Publications, 1977.

HIDDEN FIGURES

A regular polygon is one whose *sides* are all equal (congruent) and whose *angles* are all equal (congruent). In the drawing below, locate four regular polygons: a triangle, a quadrilateral (square), a pentagon (five sides), and a hexagon (six sides).

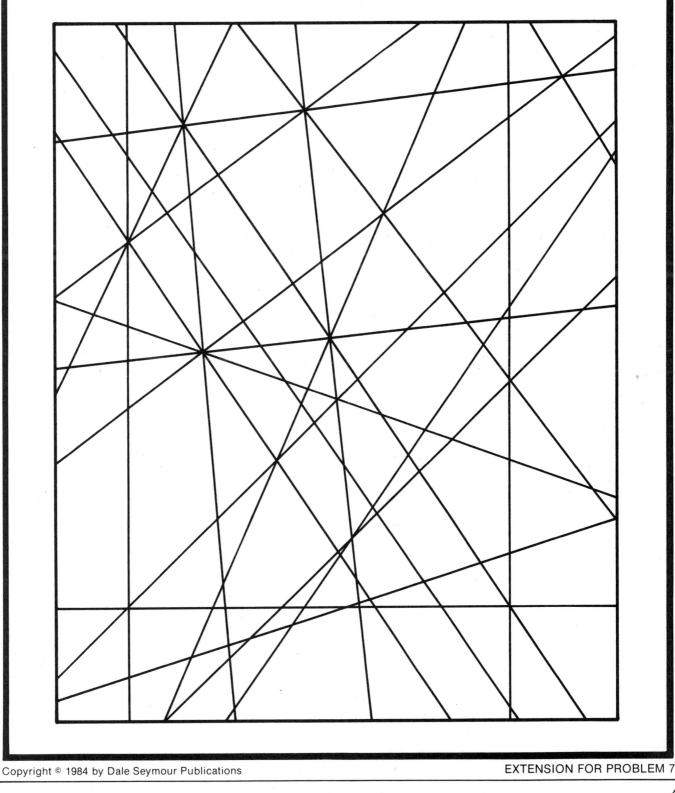

EXTENSION FOR PROBLEM 7

HIDDEN FIGURES

Answer

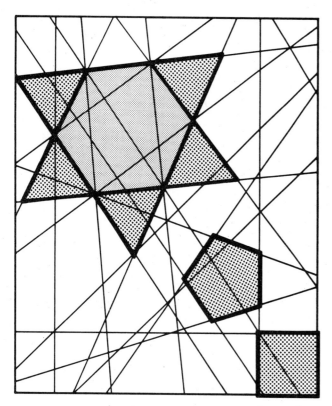

About the Problem

Depending upon the mathematics background of your students, you may need to define and discuss the concepts of polygons, regular polygons, and congruence.

Be prepared to hand out additional copies of the grid to students who make mistakes and want to start again with clean sheets.

Getting Started

Suggest that students look for the equilateral triangle first, partly because that is the simplest figure, and also because there are several of them to be found (five surrounding the hexagon, and one large triangle that includes the hexagon).

Students may want to construct or find pictures of equilateral triangles, regular pentagons, and regular hexagons, so that they know clearly what overall shape or what specific angles they are looking for among the crisscrossed lines.

If students are having trouble, remind them to be careful not to let the *size* of one discovered figure prevent them from spotting shapes either much larger or much smaller (an easy perceptual trap to fall into).

Using a colored pencil to shade in figures as they are discovered can help students keep track of them until they have time to check the lengths of their sides (and possibly their angles) for congruence.

Solution

We generally do better looking for one type of figure at a time. Students may start with the triangles for the reasons given above, or they may prefer to start looking for the square, which is probably the most familiar and easily recognized shape.

If students find and shade in all or most of the triangles, the hexagon should be obvious.

Going Beyond

A good way for students to learn more about polygons and regular polygons is through compass and straightedge activities. For ideas, see *Creative Constructions* by Dale Seymour and Reuben Schadler, Palo Alto, Calif.: Creative Publications, Inc., 1974.

PATTERN SEARCH

Find a common pattern in each
set of numbers below.

1.

34   45   78

123   678   89

2.

34   43   223

70   61   52   16

1222   331   1111111

3.

46   68   97

20   35   75   13

4.

50   35   15

145   29467310

700065

5.

93   552   66

105303   2226

110011800

6.

343   7887   21212

55   67076   27772

7.

19   31   515   142

617   501   11111

821812   91

8.

7   9   21

33   101   455   87

2468107   135791113

9.

7321   4520   6848

7963   3412   5525

236   313   9981

10.

75   641   975

5320   54

975430   876543210

Discussion for
PATTERN SEARCH

Answers

1. Each number consists of consecutive digits (increasing from left to right).
2. Each number has the digit sum of 7.
3. In each number, the difference between the digits is 2.
4. Each number is a multiple of 5 (easily spotted by the fact that all end in 0 or 5).
5. Each number has the digit sum of 12.
6. All are palindromic numbers (they read same forward or backward).
7. Each number contains the digit 1.
8. All are odd numbers.
9. In each number, the *last* two digits are the product of the *first* two digits. (7321: 7 × 3 = 21)
10. In each number, the digits are in descending order (not consecutive—but each digit is *less* than the digit to its left).

About the Problems

This set of problems was designed to make students more pattern-conscious. Some of these may be difficult for your students, but given enough time, they should have success with most of the sets. In some cases, an answer different from the one listed above may be true. If true, it should not be rejected as wrong. For example, a student might say that each number in problem 4 ends with zero or five—which is correct.

Getting Started

Suggest that students look for the "easiest" pattern first (this will vary from student to student), then jump around looking for others they recognize, rather than starting with problem 1 and proceeding sequentially to problem 10. Explain that solving one pattern may give them ideas for solving others.

Solutions

Some students, already becoming pattern-conscious, may find that patterns seem to emerge spontaneously if they simply look at the set of numbers long enough.

Other students, those with less well-developed number intuition, might find it helpful to make an organized list of as many different types of patterns as they can think of. Using this list for ideas, they can then check each number in a given set against a pattern that they guess might apply.

Such a list (showing many different pattern types) can help students break out of a mind-set that traps them into looking only for certain elements among a set of numbers.

Going Beyond

If students seem to enjoy these problems, have them design some pattern problems of their own.

WHAT'S MY NAME GAME

Find each of these two-digit numbers.

1.
The sum of my digits is 2. I'm greater than 12. Who am I?

———

2.
The sum of my digits is 10. Their difference is 2. I'm less than 50. Who am I?

———

3.
My digits are the same. Their sum is 3 less than their product. Who am I?

———

4.
The product of my digits is 10. I'm an even number. Who am I?

———

5.
The sum of my digits is the same as the product of my digits. Who am I?

———

6.
My tens digit is 1 more than my units digit. I am odd. I'm divisible by 5. Who am I?

———

7.
I'm the largest two-digit number whose units digit divides its tens digit evenly. Who am I?

———

8.
One of my digits is odd. One is even. Their product is less than 24 but greater than 18. What *two* numbers might I be?

——— ———

PROBLEM 8

WHAT'S MY NAME GAME

Answers
1. 20	5. 22		
2. 46	6. 65		
3. 33	7. 99		
4. 52	8. 45 or 54		

About the Problems

Students usually like these problems. They combine logic skills and knowledge of number concepts. One advantage of this kind of problem is that the answer is easily verified. The student simply has to test his or her answer against each of the problem statements.

The problems also provide a good test for mathematics vocabulary.

Getting Started

Students often find it helpful to make brief lists of numbers that meet the criteria for each piece of information. They then look for common numbers in each list.

Solutions

1. Sum of digits is 2: could be 11, 20. Greater than 12: eliminates 11. Answer is 20.

2. Sum of digits is 10: could be 19, 28, 37, 46, 55, 64, 73, 82, 91. Their difference is 2: eliminates all but 46 and 64. Less than 50: eliminates 64. Answer is 46.

3. Digits are the same: could be 11, 22, 33, 44, 55, 66, 77, 88, 99. Their sum is 3 less than their product:

NUMBER	SUM	PRODUCT	DIFFERENCE	
11	2	1	1	
22	4	4	0	
33	6	9	3	ANSWER
44	8	16	8	
55	10	25	15	
66	12	36	24	
77	14	49	35	
88	16	64	48	
99	18	81	63	

(Students can stop when they find that 33 meets all the criteria, unless they want to check for a second possible solution.)

4. Product of digits is 10: could be 25, 52. An even number: eliminates 25. Answer is 52.

5. Sum of digits is same as product: there are lots of combinations to check, but most students will soon come to 2 × 2 = 2 + 2. Answer is 22.

6. Tens digit is one more than units digit: could be 10, 21, 32, 43, 54, 65, 76, 87, 98. Odd number: leaves 21, 43, 65, and 87. Divisible by 5: eliminates 21, 43, and 87. Answer is 65.

7. Two-digit number whose units digit divides tens digit evenly: could be 11, 21, 31, 41, 51, 61, 71, 81, 91, 22, 42, 62, 82, 33, 63, 93, 44, 84, 55, 66, 77, 88, 99. Largest of these is 99. Answer is 99. (Students might *start* with the largest possible two-digit number. Since that's the answer, they would avoid having to list all the others.)

8. Product less than 24 but greater than 18: What two numbers have a product of 19, 20, 21, 22, or 23? Only (3 × 7) and (4 × 5). But 3 and 7 are *both* odd, so answer is 45 or 54.

Going Beyond

Once again, this is the type of problem that students enjoy creating themselves. It is good to set some parameters, such as limiting them to two-digit or three-digit numbers. Otherwise, students may make their problems too difficult for others in the class to solve.

FIND THEM ALL

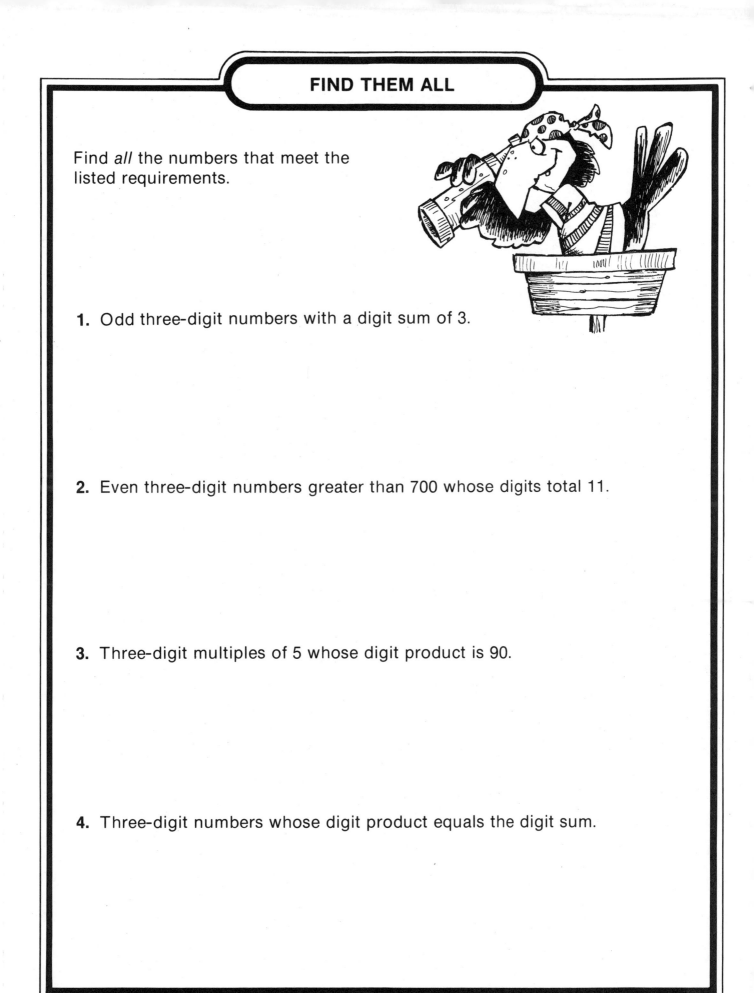

Find *all* the numbers that meet the
listed requirements.

1. Odd three-digit numbers with a digit sum of 3.

2. Even three-digit numbers greater than 700 whose digits total 11.

3. Three-digit multiples of 5 whose digit product is 90.

4. Three-digit numbers whose digit product equals the digit sum.

EXTENSION FOR PROBLEM 8

Discussion for

FIND THEM ALL

Answers

1. 111, 201
2. 704, 722, 740, 812, 830, 902, 920
3. 295, 365, 635, 925
4. 123, 132, 213, 231, 312, 321

About the Problems

These problems require a more thorough search than those in *What's My Name Game* since there are several numbers that meet each requirement. Students need to do some careful sequencing and organized listing in order to insure that all possible solutions have been considered.

Getting Started

Students who have worked *Pattern Search* or *What's My Name Game* should have no difficulty getting started with these. They will, however, need to be thorough and careful to find *all* solutions.

Solutions

The combinations here are simple, so all arithmetic should be mental. One approach is to make complete lists of numbers that meet one of the criteria, then go back through the list eliminating numbers that don't meet the other criteria.

1. Digit sum of 3: could be 111, 201, 210, 300. Must be *odd*: eliminates 210 and 300. Answers are 111, 201.

2. Digit sum of 11, where first digit is 7 or greater: could be
   704, 713, 722, 731, 740
   803, 812, 821, 830
   902, 911, 920
   Must be *even*: eliminates 713, 731, 803, 821, and 911. Answers are all those that remain.

3. Digit product of 90: factors of 90 are (2, 5, 9) and (3, 5, 6). So, possible numbers are: 259, 295, 356, 365, 536, 563, 635, 653, 925, 952. Must be multiple of 5: eliminates all but 295, 365, 635, and 925.

4. This is a difficult problem because there is no obvious place to start. We need to set up some organized system that will help us find the answer without checking 999 separate numbers. One approach would be to start with the first two digits constant, the third changing.
   111 112 113 114 115 . . . 119
   None of these fit the criteria.
   (121) 122 123 124 125 . . . 129
   We can skip 121 because we already tried a permutation of it (112). 123 is the first number that works: 1 + 2 + 3 = 6 and 1 × 2 × 3 = 6. We know that all permutations of those three digits, then, will also meet the criteria: 123, 132, 213, 231, 312, and 321.

   As we continue checking to see if there are additional answers, we soon learn that the digits must all be fairly small, because larger digits always have products that far exceed their sums. Soon we are satisfied that the six answers we found are the only ones that meet the criteria.

Going Beyond

Once again, students will enjoy and benefit from creating their own problems and solutions similar to these.

DART TOURNEY

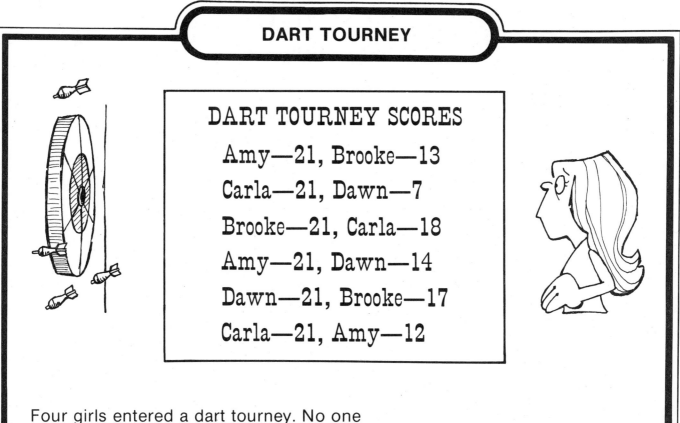

DART TOURNEY SCORES
Amy—21, Brooke—13
Carla—21, Dawn—7
Brooke—21, Carla—18
Amy—21, Dawn—14
Dawn—21, Brooke—17
Carla—21, Amy—12

Four girls entered a dart tourney. No one went undefeated. It was decided that the winner would be the one with the highest total points scored.

Who won? _____

How many points did she score? _____

Find each girl's *average* score per game:

Amy's average _____

Brooke's average _____

Carla's average _____

Dawn's average _____

WARM-UP FOR PROBLEM 9

Discussion for

DART TOURNEY

Answers

Carla won with 60 points.

Amy's average: 18 points
Brooke's average: 17 points
Carla's average: 20 points
Dawn's average: 14 points

About the Problem

This problem is designed to make students organize data and figure averages (arithmetic mean). Scores were selected to give nondecimal answers.

Getting Started

Students should not need help on this problem. They need only to be careful about including *all* the scores for each girl as they find the totals.

Solution

Total points scored (to find winner)
Carla: 21 + 21 + 18 = 60 points
Amy: 21 + 21 + 12 = 54 points
Brooke: 21 + 13 + 17 = 51 points
Dawn: 21 + 7 + 14 = 42 points

Averages
Carla: 60 ÷ 3 = 20 points
Amy: 54 ÷ 3 = 18 points
Brooke: 51 ÷ 3 = 17 points
Dawn: 42 ÷ 3 = 14 points

Going Beyond

A similar problem that requires decimal answers is as follows:

Four boys held a dart tourney. Their scores are given below. What was each boy's average score?

Brad–21, Alex–7
David–21, Clint–10
Brad–21, Clint–13
Alex–21, David–17
David–21, Brad–20
Clint–21, Alex–15

Answers
Alex: 14.3 point average
Brad: 20.7 point average
Clint: 14.7 point average
David: 19.7 point average

WHAT'S THE SCORE?

The average of Anne's, Sara's, and Julie's test scores is 72. Julie scored 100 and Anne scored 10 points higher than Sara. What were Anne's and Sara's scores?

PROBLEM 9

Discussion for
WHAT'S THE SCORE

Answer Anne scored 63 points.
Sara scored 53 points.

About the Problem

This problem requires an understanding of the concept of *average* (arithmetic mean). Students will need to read the problem carefully.

Getting Started

If students need a hint, suggest that they "think backwards" from what the *sum* of the three scores would be, given an average score of 72.

Solution

If the average of the three scores is 72, then the total of the three scores is 3 × 72, or 216. Julie scored 100 points, so the sum of Anne and Sara's scores is 216 minus 100, or 116 points. If Anne and Sara had scored exactly the same, they would have each scored 116 ÷ 2, or 58 points. Since Anne scored 10 points more than Sara, add 5 points to 58 to find Anne's score (63), and subtract 5 points from 58 for Sara's score (53). A check shows that:

53 + 63 + 100 = 216 (total points)

216 ÷ 3 = 72 (average score)

Going Beyond

When students were unable to work the problem successfully but seem to have understood the explanation of the solution, give them a chance to try again.

Tell them to substitute the average score 84 for 72 in the problem. All other facts remain the same.

Solution

3 × 84 = 252 (total points scored)

252 – 100 = 152 points (total of Anne's and Sara's scores)

152 ÷ 2 = 76 points (average of Anne's and Sara's scores)

76 + 5 = 81 points (Anne's score)

76 – 5 = 71 points (Sara's score)

Check: 71 + 81 + 100 = 252 ÷ 3 = 84 points (average)

BATTING AVERAGES

On July 10, both Bill and Mario had a batting average of .250. Bill had 10 hits in 40 times at bat. Mario had 12 hits in 48 times at bat. If each of them gets 2 hits in 2 times at bat in their next game, what will their new batting averages be?

EXTENSION FOR PROBLEM 9

BATTING AVERAGES

Answer   Bill's new average is .286.
Mario's new average is .280.

About the Problem

This is a challenging problem for students unfamiliar with batting averages.

Getting Started

Be sure that students understand how batting averages are computed: number of hits divided by number of times at bat. They also need to know that batting averages are rounded to three decimal places.

Have the students restate the problem in their own words. Hints: What is each batter's new number of hits? What is his new number of at bats?

Solution

Bill gets two more hits in two more times at bat, so his new number of total *hits* is 12, and his new number of *at bats* is 42.

batting average = number of hits ÷ number of at bats

12 ÷ 42 = .2857142 = .286 (rounded)

Mario gets two more hits in two more times at bat, so his new number of hits is 14 and his new number of at bats is 50.

14 ÷ 50 = .280

Going Beyond

It is worthwhile to point out to students that although Bill and Mario both had the same average originally (.250), and they both got the same number of hits (2 for 2) in the next game, their averages are now different. Why? (They each had a different number of total *at bats*.)

A good exercise with averages is to find a current team batting average for a favorite local team as listed in the sports page, and to follow the changes in that average over a week's period.

Suppose you could rearrange the three digits on each of these license plates. Which plate would make the number with the greatest value? The number with the least value?

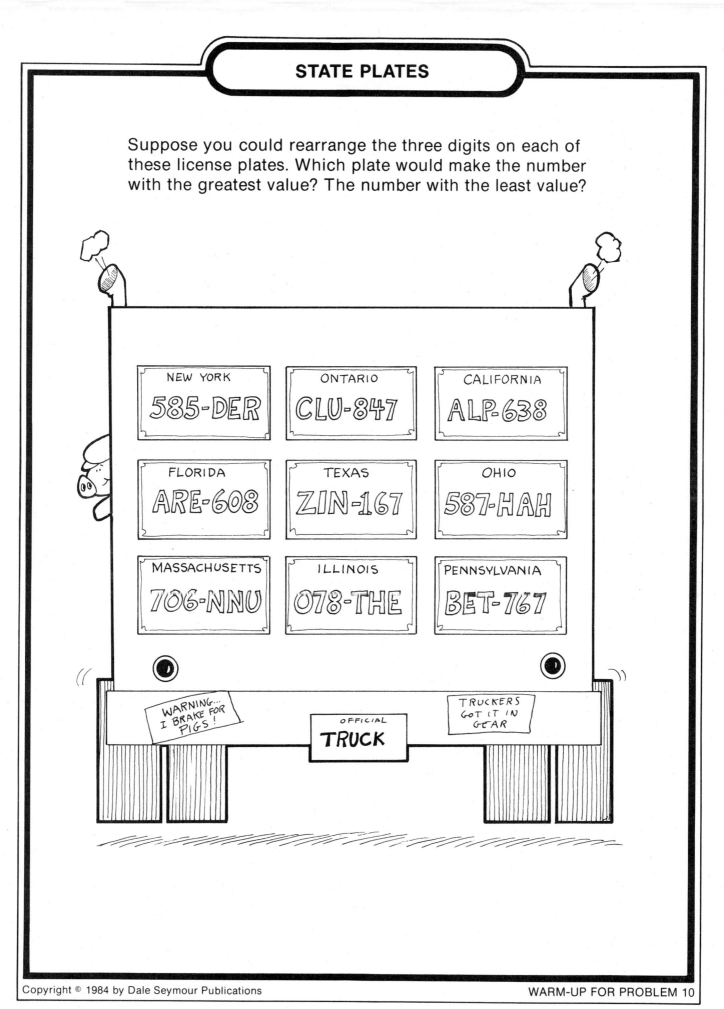

Discussion for

STATE PLATES

Answers

The digits on the Ohio plate, 587-HAH, can be re-arranged to 875, the greatest possible number.
The digits on the Massachusetts plate, 706-NNU, can be rearranged to 067, the least possible number.

About the Problem

This is an easy problem that has some interesting expansion possibilities (see *Going Beyond*). License plates are part of the students' everyday world and are a natural resource for interesting combination problems.

Getting Started

Be sure that students understand that, in finding the number with the least value, they are allowed to make a number with zero in the hundreds place—something that is normally not allowed, but is necessary with license plates that have three assigned digits.

Solutions

To find the number with the greatest value, we first look for the greatest digit that could fill the hundreds place. There is no 9, but there are several 8's. Possible plates are:

New York: 585
Ontario: 847
California: 638
Florida: 608
Ohio: 587
Illinois: 078

Of these, the plates with the greatest digit left for the tens place (7) are Ontario, Ohio, and Illinois. Of these, the Ohio plate has the greatest digit left for the units place (5).

By a similar process, we look for the number with the least value in the plates with 0:

Florida: 608
Massachusetts: 706
Illinois: 078

The least digits for the hundreds place and units place are found in the Massachusetts plate.

Going Beyond

You can use the same nine plates for some extension problems. Which digits on the license plates already are, or could be rearranged to make, the following:

a. a multiple of 5?
b. an even number?
c. a palindromic number?
d. a multiple of 3?
e. a multiple of 9?
f. a composite number?

Answers

a. The New York plate, both as is (585) and changed to 855.
   The Florida plate changed to 680 or 860.
   The Ohio plate changed to 875 or 785.
   The Massachusetts plate changed to 760 or 670.
   The Illinois plate changed to 780 or 870.
b. Each of the plates can be changed to an even number.
c. The New York plate has a palindromic number (585) as does the Pennsylvania plate (767).
d. The New York and Illinois plates are (and can be changed to) multiples of 3.
e. The New York plate is (and can be changed to) a multiple of 9.
f. All the plates are now or can be rearranged to make even numbers (divisible by 2) and thus composite numbers.

List all the different four-digit whole numbers that can be written using the digits 1, 3, 5, and 7. Use each digit only once in a number.

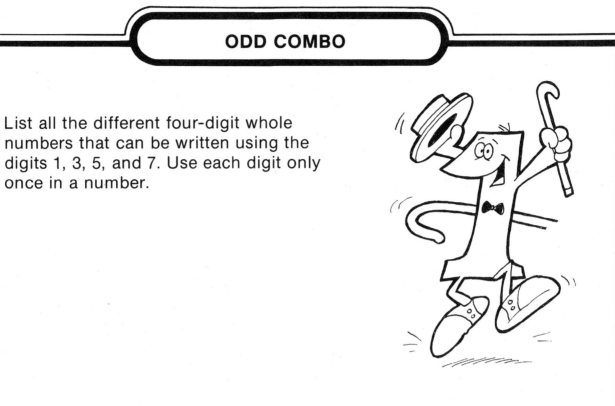

Discussion for

ODD COMBO

Answers

1357	3157	5137	7135
1375	3175	5173	7153
1537	3517	5317	7315
1573	3571	5371	7351
1735	3715	5713	7513
1753	3751	5731	7531

About the Problem

This combination problem leads students to practice the techniques of making a list that keeps certain digits constant while alternating others, which is a valuable problem-solving skill.

Getting Started

Students will need to make an organized list. Without such a systematic listing, they may overlook some answers. If students seem to have trouble getting started, giving them a list of the first few numbers may help them discover a pattern to follow.

Solution

It is interesting to see how students who have never been asked to make this kind of list will approach the problem. It is not important whether they start with the greatest or the least number, just so they have a system that covers all possible combinations. The answers listed above demonstrate a system in which the first digit is kept constant while the next three are alternated. Some students may come up with the same system but in reverse—keeping the last digit constant and alternating the first three.

Going Beyond

Give students a similar problem; for example:

List all the three-digit numbers that can be written using the digits 2, 4, or 6. *Digits can be repeated in a number.*

Answers

222	422	622
224	424	624
226	426	626
242	442	642
244	444	644
246	446	646
262	462	662
264	464	664
266	466	666

There are four possible scoring plays in an NFL football game:

Touchdown	6 points
Point after touchdown	1 point
Field goal	3 points
Safety	2 points

1. List all the ways that a team could score 11 points.

2. What final scores for one team are *not* possible?

3. If the 2-point safety did not exist, what scores would *not* be possible?

4. If the 3-point field goal did not exist, what scores would *not* be possible?

5. What scores *cannot* be made if a team doesn't score a safety or a field goal?

EXTENSION FOR PROBLEM 10

WINNING COMBINATIONS

Answers

1. 6 pts + 3 pts + 2 pts = 11 pts
   6 pts + 2 pts + 2 pts + 1 pt = 11 pts
   3 pts + 3 pts + 3 pts + 2 pts = 11 pts
   3 pts + 2 pts + 2 pts + 2 pts + 2 pts = 11 pts
2. 1 pt
3. 1 pt, 2 pts, 4 pts, 5 pts, 8 pts, 11 pts
4. 1 pt, 3 pts, 5 pts
5. 1 pt, 2 pts, 3 pts, 4 pts, 5 pts, 8 pts, 9 pts, 10 pts, 11 pts, 15 pts, 16 pts, 17 pts, 22 pts, 23 pts, 29 pts

About the Problem

These problems require some careful organization for complete solutions.

Getting Started

Make it clear that 1 point can be scored *only* following a touchdown.

Solutions

As with other combination problems, a systematic listing is needed to find all the answers. In problem 1, we try all possible combinations of 6, 3, 1, and 2 that add to 11, aware that every 1 must be paired with a 6. In problems 2–5, we simply test the numbers one by one, starting with 1, mentally checking to see which can and which can't be obtained by summing combinations of the allowable digits.

Going Beyond

Other interesting ways to extend the exploration of combinations are as follows:

1. List all the combinations that can be thrown with a pair of fair dice.
2. Maria has three blouses that go well with four skirts. How many different combinations can she wear?
3. Four boys (*A, B, C,* and *D*) ran a race. How many different ways can they finish?

Problems like these often involve the important question of whether or not order is important. When order is *not* important in a grouping or arrangement, then we are working with *combinations*. When order is important, as in the boys' race, then the arrangements are called *permutations*.

MISSING DIGITS

Fill in the boxes with single-digit
numbers that will make a correct
computation problem.

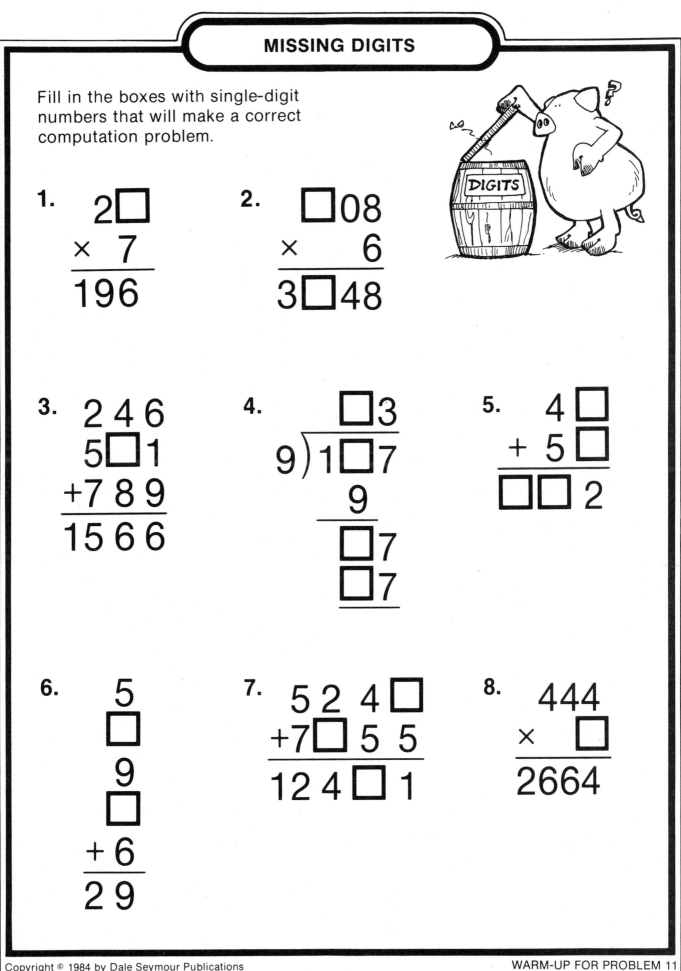

1.
```
   2 ☐
 ×   7
 ─────
 1 9 6
```

2.
```
   ☐ 0 8
 ×     6
 ───────
 3 ☐ 4 8
```

3.
```
   2 4 6
   5 ☐ 1
 + 7 8 9
 ───────
 1 5 6 6
```

4.
```
        ☐ 3
   9 ) 1 ☐ 7
        9
       ───
        ☐ 7
        ☐ 7
       ───
```

5.
```
     4 ☐
 +   5 ☐
 ───────
 ☐ ☐ 2
```

6.
```
     5
     ☐
     9
     ☐
 +   6
 ─────
   2 9
```

7.
```
   5 2 4 ☐
 + 7 ☐ 5 5
 ─────────
 1 2 4 ☐ 1
```

8.
```
   4 4 4
 ×     ☐
 ───────
 2 6 6 4
```

Discussion for
MISSING DIGITS

Answers

Answers to problems 2, 5, and 6 may vary. See other answers in *Solutions*.

1. 2⟦8⟧
    × 7
    ───
    196

2. ⟦5⟧08
    × 6
    ────
    3⟦0⟧48

3. 246
    5⟦3⟧1
    +789
    ────
    1566

4. ⟦1⟧3
    9)1⟦1⟧7
      9
    ───
     2⟦7⟧
     2⟦7⟧

5. 4⟦7⟧
    +5⟦5⟧
    ────
    ⟦10⟧2

6. 5
    ⟦7⟧
    9
    ⟦2⟧
    +6
    ──
    29

7. 524⟦6⟧
    +7⟦1⟧55
    ─────
    124⟦0⟧1

8. 444
    × ⟦6⟧
    ────
    2664

About the Problem

These problems test the students' logic as well as their understanding of the basic facts and properties of numbers. Unlike most problems of this type, the problems here are fairly easy. Success with these problems will help provide the confidence needed to solve more complex problems, like the ones that follow in *Even Sum* and *Alphamath*.

Getting Started

If necessary, suggest that students begin with trial-and-error techniques. They will quite naturally work into a logical approach when their guesses don't work.

Solutions

In every problem, no matter how students arrive at their answers, they should check them by performing the computation.

1. We might solve this problem by dividing 196 by 7. An alternative approach is to ask, "What single digit multiplied by 7 gives an answer that ends in 6?" 8 × 7 = 56, so we try 8 in the blank.

2. The problem here can be simplified to 6 × __ = 3__, as the units and tens digits are irrelevant. We think, "What number multiplied by 6 gives us an answer in the 30's?" Possible answers are 5 and 6. A check shows that either will work with the given problem: 6 × 508 = 3048, or 6 × 608 = 3648.

3. We add the units: 6 + 1 + 9 = 16, carry 1 to the tens. Adding the tens: 1 + 4 + 8 = 13. We need a sum that ends in 6, such as 16, so we try 3 in the blank. A check shows that 3 works.

4. The first digit in the quotient must be 1 because 1 × 9 = 9 (given). The missing digit *below* must be 2, because 3 × 9 = 27 (there is no remainder). That means the missing digit in the dividend must be 1, because 11 – 9 = 2.

5. The first two missing digits in the answer must be 10, because in adding only two digits, we can't possibly carry more than 1 ten, and 4 + 5 + 1 = 10. The units digits must then be any two digits that total 12. (They can't total only 2, because we need to carry 1 ten.) Possible digits are 6 and 6, 7 and 5, 8 and 4, or 9 and 3. A check shows that all combinations of those will work: 46 + 56 = 102; 47 + 55 = 102; 45 + 57 = 102; 48 + 54 = 102; 44 + 58 = 102; 49 + 53 = 102.

6. We might approach this by adding 5 + 9 + 6 = 20, and subtracting 29 – 20 = 9. This way we learn that the two missing digits must together equal 9. Possible answers are 5 and 4, 6 and 3, 7 and 2, or 8 and 1. (9 and 0 is not a likely pair, as we rarely see 0 as a single digit in an addition problem.) A check shows that any of these pairs will work.

7. Starting with the units: what number plus 5 equals 11? (We know the sum is not 21, because 21 – 5 = 16, which is a two-digit number.) The missing digit must be 6. We carry 1 ten: 1 + 4 + 5 = 10, so the missing digit in the tens must be 0. We carry 1 hundred: 1 + 2 + ? = 4. The missing hundreds digit must be 1. A check shows we are right.

8. As with problem 1, we might solve this by dividing 2664 by 444. It is probably easier, though, to consider the given units digits and think, "What single digit multiplied by 4 gives an answer that ends in 4?" 6 × 4 = 24, so we try 6 in the blank, then multiply and check.

Going Beyond

Ask students which answers are *unique*—that is, the only possible answers. The concept of uniqueness is very important in mathematics. Good problem-solvers need to learn to consider the uniqueness of answers early in their mathematics education. (Problems 1, 3, 4, 7, and 8 have unique answers.)

Each letter represents a number. When a letter is used more than once, it represents the same number. EVEN is an even number. ODD is an odd number. Can you find two solutions?

$$\begin{array}{r} ODD \\ + ODD \\ \hline EVEN \end{array}$$

PROBLEM 11

Discussion for
EVEN SUM

Answers

```
 655     855
+655    +855
────    ────
1310    1710
```

About the Problem

For many students, this problem may be more difficult than most of the others in *Problem Parade*. It requires students to use deductive logic. It is a good problem, and students should see some patterns that provide clues to the solution.

Getting Started

Let students work on the problem awhile before giving *any* clues. The very process of discovering the clues is exciting, so give students the chance to experience this excitement, and provide help or hints only if they are completely stuck. Give only one clue at a time, as a single clue may suggest to students the approach required to solve the problem, even though other insights or discoveries are still needed in order to solve the problem.

Some hints you might give are as follows:

1. If the sum of the two three-digit numbers is a four-digit number, the three-digit numbers have to be *at least* how great? (*500*)
2. If the sum of D + D is N in the units place and E in the tens place, is the sum of D + D 10 or greater? (*yes*)
3. Since the four-digit number starts with E, what number do you think E is? (*1, because O + O would have to be between 10 and 19.*)

Solution

The deductive solution takes several steps; no specific order is necessary. One possible step-by-step approach is as follows:

1. Since O + O equals a two-digit number, O is 5 or greater.
2. Since O + O equals EV, or (if 1 was carried from the tens place) 1 less than EV, then E must be 1.
3. Since ODD is odd, then D must be odd.
4. Since D + D equals N in the units and E in the tens, there must be a 1 carried to the tens place to make E different from N.
5. Since E is 1, then N must be 1 less, or 0 (zero).
6. If N is 0, then D must be 5. (5 + 5 = 10)
7. Candidates for ODD are now limited to 655, 755, 855, and 955.
8. 655 gives a solution.
   755 doesn't work because V is 5 and D is 5. (Can't be.)
   855 gives a solution.
   955 doesn't work because V is 9 and O is 9. (Can't be.)
9. Conclusion: There are only two solutions (see *Answers*).

Going Beyond

Some students will love these problems; others will think they are too hard. If you select more problems like this, try them yourself first to be sure they are not too difficult for your students. Several fairly easy ones appear in the extension problems of *Alphamath*.

ALPHAMATH

In each of these problems, letters represent single-digit numbers. If a letter is used more than once, it represents the same number *in that problem.* How many solutions can you find?

1.
$$
\begin{array}{r}
AAA \\
+BBB \\
\hline
CCC
\end{array}
$$

2.
$$
\begin{array}{r}
MMM \\
NNN \\
+PPP \\
\hline
QQQ
\end{array}
$$

3.
$$
\begin{array}{r}
TTT \\
\times\ \ \ S \\
\hline
RRR
\end{array}
$$

4.
$$
\begin{array}{r}
AA\ \ \\
A\overline{)CBA} \\
CA\ \ \\
\hline
CA\ \ \\
CA\ \ \\
\hline
\end{array}
$$

5.
$$
\begin{array}{r}
MM\ \ \ \\
MM\overline{)ABCD} \\
AED\ \ \\
\hline
AED\ \ \\
AED\ \ \\
\hline
\end{array}
$$

6.
$$
\begin{array}{r}
WWW \\
-\ \ YY \\
\hline
QZ
\end{array}
$$

7.
$$
\begin{array}{r}
ABC \\
+DEF \\
\hline
GHI
\end{array}
$$

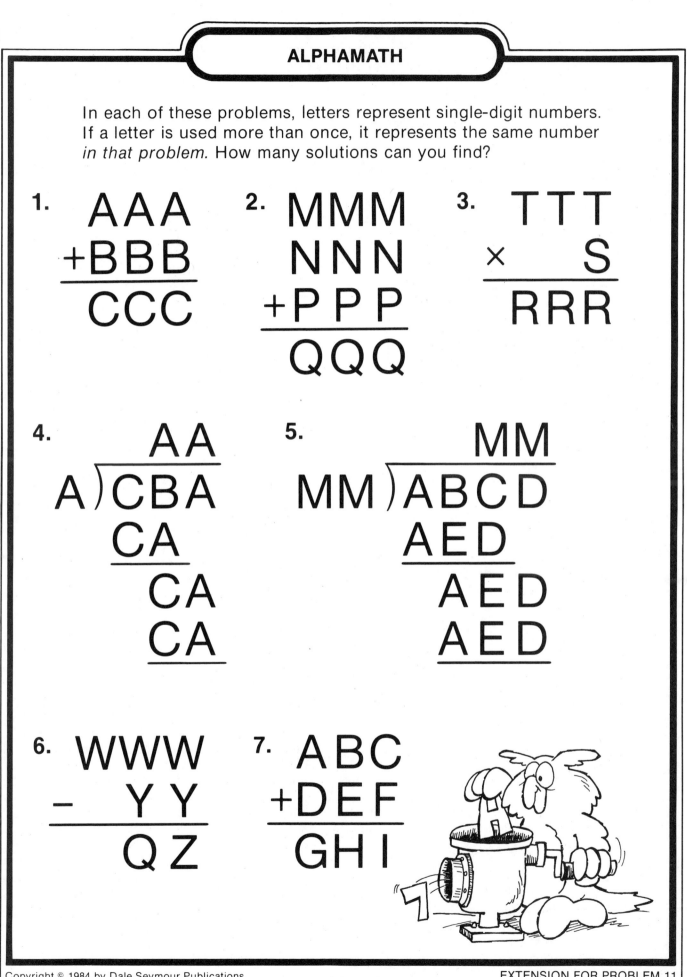

EXTENSION FOR PROBLEM 11

ALPHAMATH

Answers

1. There are 32 different answers. Samples:

111	222	333	444	555	666	777	888
+222	+111	+111	+111	+111	+111	+111	+111
333	333	444	555	666	777	888	999

2. Assuming that none of the digits are zero (as 000 is rarely seen in addition problems), there are 42 answers. If we allow 000, there are 94 additional answers. Samples:

111	111	111	000	111	111
222	222	222	111	000	222
333	444	555	222	222	000
666	777	888	333	333	333

3.
333	444	222	222
× 2	× 2	× 3	× 4
666	888	666	888

4.
```
      55            66           5.       44
  5) 275        6) 396            44) 1936
    25            36                    176
    25            36                    176
    25  .         36                    176
```

6.
111	111	111	111	111	111
− 22	− 33	− 44	− 66	− 77	− 88
89	78	67	45	34	23

7. There are numerous answers. Samples:

234	675	267
+567	+243	+534
801	918	801

About the Problems

The seven problems are arranged in general order of difficulty. Students will probably gain confidence by solving the easier problems first. Finding one answer for any problem can be done by using a guess-and-test approach. Finding *all* the answers for a single problem will require some organized listing and additional use of logic.

Getting Started

If students have worked on the two preceding problems (*Missing Digits* and *Even Sum*), they should have no trouble getting started on these. Be sure students understand the rules: that a letter is always the same digit within a problem, although it may be another digit in different problems, and that two different letters cannot represent the *same* digit within a problem.

Solutions

1. Starting with a simplest code, A = 1, B = 2, and C = 3, then increasing the digits one by one, we soon find that numerous possibilities will work. The only thing to watch here is not to use zero or digits that give a four-digit answer.

2. The approach here would be the same as for problem 1.

3. Using 0 or 1 as a multiplier or multiplicand would create an unallowable digit repeat. Digits larger than 2, 3, and 4 will give a four-digit product. Therefore, possible answers are limited to combinations of 2, 3, and 4.

4. We can simply test the nine possibilities for the letter A. One clue is that all three numbers—divisor, dividend, and quotient—must end with the same digit. Multiplying, we find that only 1×1, 5×5, and 6×6 yield products that satisfy this requirement.

5. As in problem 4, we could experiment with nine possibilities for the letter M. We know that M must be greater than 3 in order for M × MM to yield a three-digit partial product. Since M appears nowhere in the partial products, we can eliminate 5, 6, and 9. Neither 7 nor 8 work, because in each case two letters would have to represent the same digit. Only M = 4 will work.

6. The three-digit number must be less than 200 to avoid a three-digit difference. Therefore, we need to test only 111 for WWW. We then test the digits 2 through 9 for Y.

7. This problem has many answers. Its solution will likely be a guess-and-test procedure. There are nine letters and ten possible digits. Starting with *any* three digits in the top addend position, we can work out the second addend by testing the unused digits from right to left (starting with the units digit and adding as we go, to insure that only *new* digits appear in the sum as well).

Going Beyond

Problems like this are available in many recreational math books. However, their difficulty level is generally above that of the students for whom this book is intended. Use them with caution.

Students may enjoy designing their own problems, but be aware that it is easy for these problems to get ridiculously difficult. If, for example, a student simply makes up a computation problem and then assigns a letter-code to the digits after the fact, the problem may be too hard. While better students might enjoy discovering that there are insufficient clues to solve such problems in a reasonable amount of time, other students will only be frustrated by them. Therefore, you may want to make certain restrictions to keep the difficulty level down, such as requiring the use of repeated digits (as in the problems on this worksheet), or limiting to three or four the number of different digits that can appear in a problem.

A stoplight flashes red for 50 seconds, yellow for 5 seconds, and green for 65 seconds. For what fraction of a 24-hour day is the stoplight yellow?

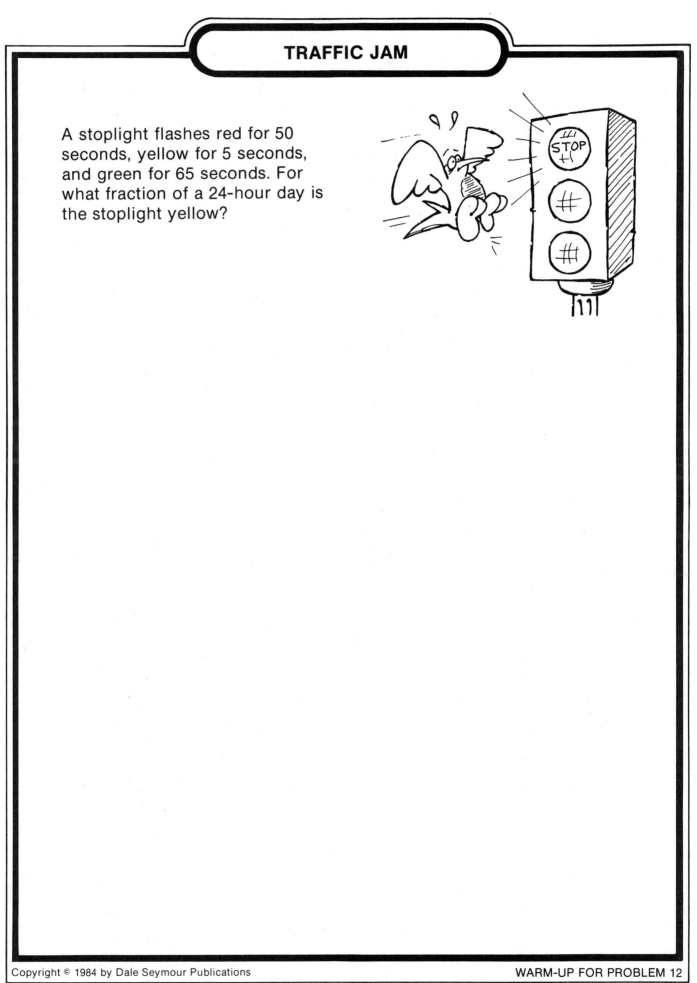

Discussion for

TRAFFIC JAM

Answer 5/120, or 1/24

About the Problem

This problem requires an understanding of fractions.

Students will need to determine what information is relevant in the problem. They are led to compare a sample period of time (2 minutes) to a longer period of time (24 hours).

Getting Started

Be sure students understand that we assume the traffic light operates 24 hours a day.

If students don't come up with a strategy after working with the problem for a while, suggest that they find the fraction of time that each color is on during one red-yellow-green cycle (*120 seconds, or 2 minutes*).

Solution

The light is yellow for 5 seconds during each red-yellow-green cycle. The cycle is 120 seconds; therefore, the light is yellow for 5/120 or 1/24 of the cycle. The cycle is continuous, so the light will be yellow for 1/24 of the time, no matter how long a time period we use: a 24-hour day, a 7-day week, a 365-day year.

Point out to students that it is *not* necessary to figure how many seconds a day the light is each color. A day is divided evenly by a single red-yellow-green cycle (2 minutes is a factor of 1440 minutes, or 24 hours), so the number of seconds each color is on during the day is the same no matter what part of the cycle is in effect the second the day begins.

Going Beyond

To emphasize the importance that the time cycle of 2 minutes "fits exactly" into the larger period of time (24 hours, or 1440 minutes), have the students consider the following problem.

George, Sonja, and Roberto work for a 24-hour security patrol. Each person has an 8-hour shift. None of their duty times overlap.

1. If George comes on duty at 8 P.M., when is he relieved? (*4 A.M.*)
2. If Sonja relieves George and works 8 straight hours, what are her hours? (*4 A.M. to 12 noon*)
3. What fraction of the day is each person on duty? (*1/3*)
4. Now, suppose the security watch were divided among four people—Abby, Boyd, Cole, and Dara—who each work 7 hours. Use a number line to show how the four would *not* work the same fraction of a single given day.

That is, Abby, Boyd, and Cole each work 7/24 of Monday, but Dara works 3/24 of Monday and 4/24 of Tuesday on her shift.

5. Discuss the difference in working 7/24 of a day in general and 7/24 of a specific day.

The tile shown here is the basic unit that makes an entire floor pattern. What fraction of the tile is white? Green? Yellow? Brown (B)?

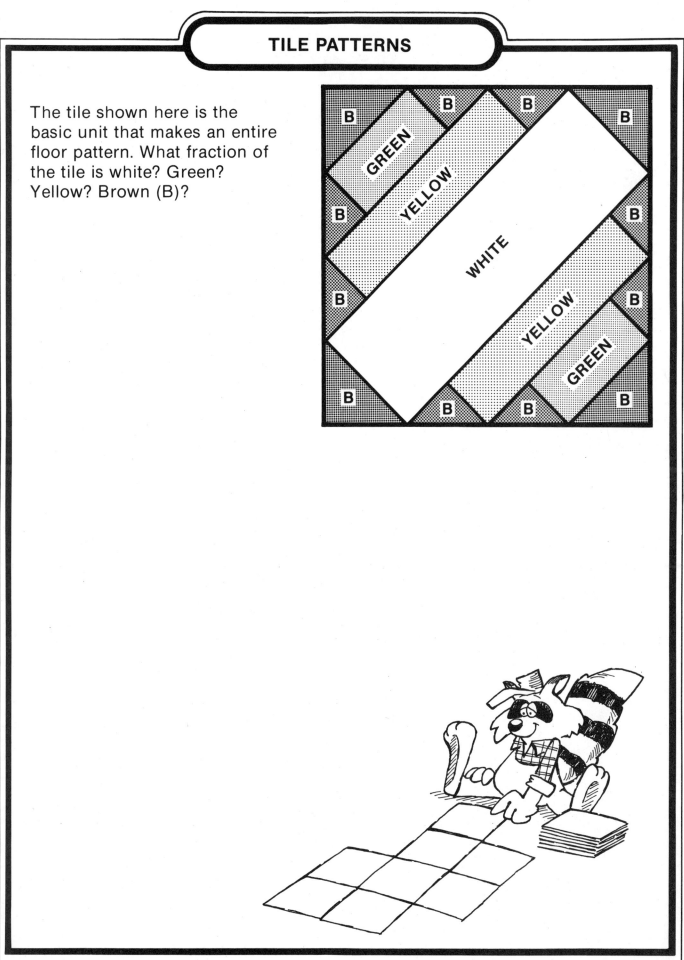

PROBLEM 12

Discussion for
TILE PATTERNS

Answers

3/8 white, 1/8 green, 1/4 yellow, 1/4 brown

About the Problem

A prerequisite for this problem is some experience in writing and simplifying fractions.

The solution to this problem will not be obvious to most students. They will have to do some sketching to divide the basic tile.

Unfortunately, students often feel that if they can't get a problem immediately, or don't even see an approach to take immediately, then they can't solve the problem. We need to give them more problems like this one that they can explore over a period of time.

Getting Started

Before suggesting to students (as a hint) that they connect points or extend lines to divide up the tile into equal parts, let them play with the problem. Given enough time, they might come up with that idea themselves. If they still need help after they have struggled awhile, give them the hint.

Solution

If we extend the given lines and connect corners, we can divide the figure into congruent unit squares. The triangular sections around the perimeter are half the size of the squares.

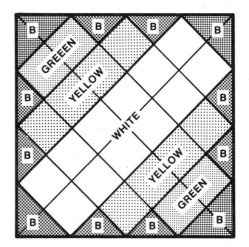

In terms of unit squares, there are 32 in the entire tile. Twelve of these are white, four are green, eight are yellow, and eight are brown. This gives the following fractional amounts:

    white: 12/32, or 3/8 of the square
    green: 4/32, or 1/8 of the square
    yellow: 8/32, or 1/4 of the square
    brown: 8/32, or 1/4 of the square

Going Beyond

Suggest that students create their own geometric tile patterns and find the fraction of the tile that is each color. You might allow them complete freedom, or you might impose restrictions on the number of colors or number of unit squares they are allowed to use. Students can exchange their problems, or you can collect them for a set of class problems on fractions.

Maybe you've heard the statement, "A number has many names." For example, the number *one-half* can be shown in several forms:

$$\frac{1}{2} = \frac{2}{4} = \frac{3}{6} = 0.5 = 0.50 = 0.500$$

The decimal equivalent of the fraction $\frac{1}{2}$ is found by dividing 1 by 2.

```
    0.5
2)1.0
   1 0
```

We can find the decimal equivalent of $\frac{3}{8}$ by dividing 8 by 3:

```
     0.375
8)3.000
   2 4
      60
      56
       40
       40
```

$\frac{3}{8} = 0.375$

Find decimal equivalents for the following fractions:

1. $\frac{1}{4}$

2. $\frac{3}{4}$

3. $\frac{5}{8}$

4. $\frac{7}{8}$

5. $\frac{3}{16}$

6. $\frac{5}{32}$

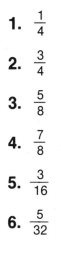

EQUIVALENTS

Answers

1. 0.25
2. 0.75
3. 0.625
4. 0.875
5. 0.1875
6. 0.15625

About the Problems

This could be an interesting enrichment worksheet for students who have not been previously introduced to decimal equivalents. If your students have already covered this concept, you may either use the problems as review or skip them entirely.

Notice that the fractions selected for the problems do not have equivalents that are repeating decimals.

Getting Started

The two examples given for finding the decimal equivalents of 1/2 and 3/8 should be sufficient to show students the process.

Solutions

1.
$$\begin{array}{r} 0.25 \\ 4\overline{)1.00} \\ 8 \\ \hline 20 \\ 20 \\ \hline \end{array}$$

2.
$$\begin{array}{r} 0.75 \\ 4\overline{)3.00} \\ 28 \\ \hline 20 \\ 20 \\ \hline \end{array}$$

3.
$$\begin{array}{r} 0.625 \\ 8\overline{)5.000} \\ 48 \\ \hline 20 \\ 16 \\ \hline 40 \\ 40 \\ \hline \end{array}$$

4.
$$\begin{array}{r} 0.875 \\ 8\overline{)7.000} \\ 64 \\ \hline 60 \\ 56 \\ \hline 40 \\ 40 \\ \hline \end{array}$$

5.
$$\begin{array}{r} 0.1875 \\ 16\overline{)3.0000} \\ 16 \\ \hline 140 \\ 128 \\ \hline 120 \\ 112 \\ \hline 80 \\ 80 \\ \hline \end{array}$$

6.
$$\begin{array}{r} 0.15625 \\ 32\overline{)5.00000} \\ 32 \\ \hline 180 \\ 160 \\ \hline 200 \\ 192 \\ \hline 80 \\ 64 \\ \hline 160 \\ 160 \\ \hline \end{array}$$

Going Beyond

This set of problems leads naturally to the discovery that some decimals terminate and others repeat. The six examples here are all terminate. To introduce repeating decimals, ask the students to find the decimal equivalent for 1/3. Performing the division (1 divided by 3), they will find that the result is "zero point three, three, three, . . . " with the 3 repeating forever. This may be an appropriate time to introduce the *vinculum*, or the bar we place over the repeating part of the decimal. Some examples of decimal equivalents that involve repeating digits are shown below, with the bar in place. Note that sometimes a single digit repeats, but other times (as for 1/7) a whole *series* of digits repeats.

$1/3 = 0.\overline{3}$

$2/3 = 0.\overline{6}$

$1/6 = 0.1\overline{6}$

$1/7 = 0.142857142857$, or $0.\overline{142857}$

$2/7 = 0.\overline{285714}$

$1/12 = 0.08\overline{3}$

DIFFERENT MEASURES

Each of the rectangles below has the *same* area.
Each of the perimeters is different.

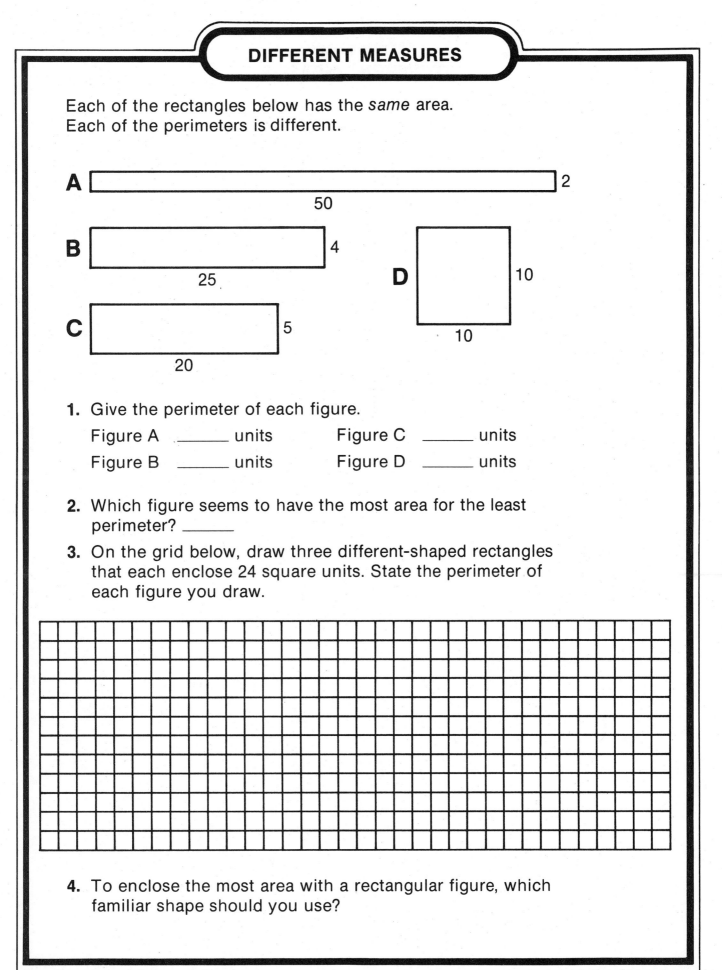

A — 50 × 2

B — 25 × 4

C — 20 × 5

D — 10 × 10

1. Give the perimeter of each figure.

   Figure A _____ units   Figure C _____ units

   Figure B _____ units   Figure D _____ units

2. Which figure seems to have the most area for the least
   perimeter? _____

3. On the grid below, draw three different-shaped rectangles
   that each enclose 24 square units. State the perimeter of
   each figure you draw.

4. To enclose the most area with a rectangular figure, which
   familiar shape should you use?

WARM-UP FOR PROBLEM 13

DIFFERENT MEASURES

Answers

1. Figure A: 104 units
   Figure B: 58 units
   Figure C: 50 units
   Figure D: 40 units
2. Figure D, the square
3. Answers will vary.
4. a square

About the Problem

This problem is designed to introduce or review the idea that perimeters of a given area can vary.

Getting Started

This warm-up worksheet may be too elementary for some students. Depending on the ability level of your students, you may or may not need to discuss the formulas for finding area and perimeter of a rectangle. You may need to remind students that area is measured in *square* units.

Solution

Perimeter is the sum of the sides of a rectangle. Students may know the formula $P = 2l + 2w$ where l and w represent length and width. Area is determined by the product of the length (l) and width (w), so the formula for finding the area of a rectangle is $A = lw$.

Going Beyond

Since a square is the rectangular shape that has the maximum area for a given perimeter, the following question is a natural extension to explore: If you had a loop of string, what shape would give the greatest area inside the string? (*a circle*) Students can explore this and suggest ideas for ways they might demonstrate the relationship.

You might also want to talk about the practice of enclosing or packaging materials in a circular shape (cylinder). Why are some packages boxes (rectangular prisms) and some cylinders?

The area of the smallest (shaded) square measures 1 square unit. What is the area of the largest square?

Discussion for

COMPARE THE SQUARES

Answer   128 square units

About the Problem

This common design provides the opportunity to explore relationships between lines, angles, shapes, and areas. It is a good, nonroutine problem that requires the solver to choose his or her own strategy for solution.

Getting Started

The best part of this problem is the time students spend thinking about how they might approach its solution. Some may do some guessing and come up with an intuitive solution. Others may try a dissection analysis, while others may fold a paper model.

We recommend that you give *no* initial hints or help to your students. If, after a while, students still don't know how to approach the problem, one of the following suggestions may help.

1. Use a piece of paper and *fold* the two smallest squares to explore their relationship.
2. Would the four triangles in the second-to-smallest square cover the smallest square exactly?

Solution

Each square has twice the area of the smaller square inscribed in it. This can be shown in four steps, using a paper model.

1. Cut a square out of paper.
2. Fold the square in half two ways to find the midpoint of each edge.
3. Connect the midpoints of adjacent sides with four more folds. This gives the inner square.
4. Show that the four triangles formed around the perimeter can be folded to fit exactly over the inscribed square.

If the first square measures 1 square unit, then the next square measures 2, the next measures 4, the next measures 8, and so on up to the largest square, which measures 128 square units.

Ask students to present any alternative approaches to solution. For example, a student familiar with the formulas for area of a square and area of a triangle might use those to show the relationships between the squares.

Going Beyond

This is a good time to introduce powers of 2. Ask students to help you complete this chart.

TRIANGLE	AREA	FACTORS OF 2	
1st	1	–	2^0
2nd	2	2	2^1
3rd	4	2×2	2^2
4th	8	$2 \times 2 \times 2$	2^3
5th	16	$2 \times 2 \times 2 \times 2$	2^4
.	.	.	.
.	.	.	.
.	.	.	.

What would the area of the 10th square be? the 20th? the 100th? the *n*th?

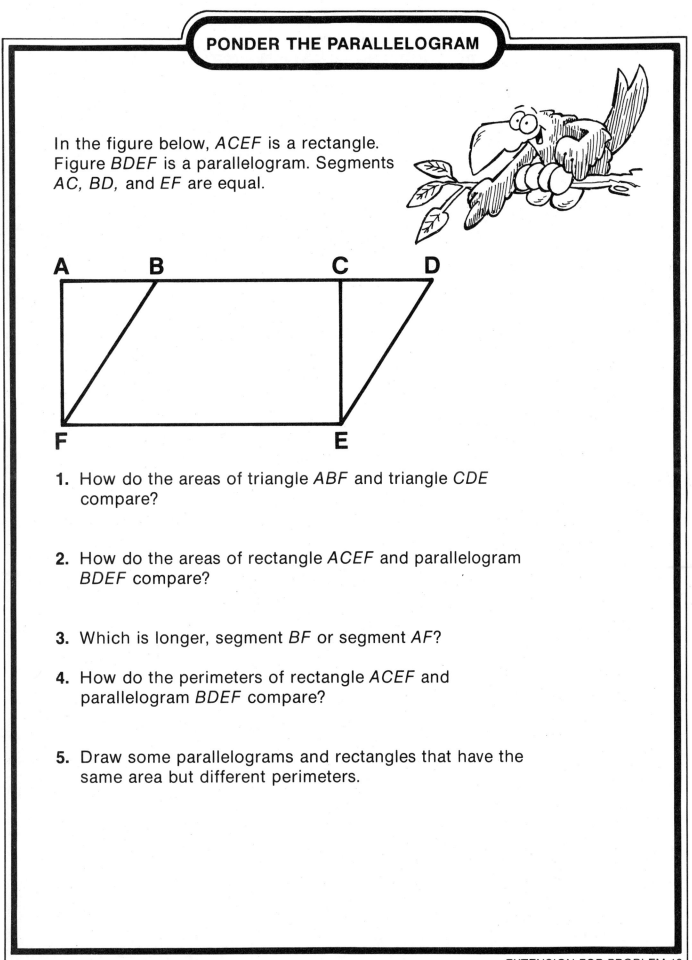

PONDER THE PARALLELOGRAM

In the figure below, *ACEF* is a rectangle. Figure *BDEF* is a parallelogram. Segments *AC, BD,* and *EF* are equal.

1. How do the areas of triangle *ABF* and triangle *CDE* compare?

2. How do the areas of rectangle *ACEF* and parallelogram *BDEF* compare?

3. Which is longer, segment *BF* or segment *AF*?

4. How do the perimeters of rectangle *ACEF* and parallelogram *BDEF* compare?

5. Draw some parallelograms and rectangles that have the same area but different perimeters.

Discussion for
PONDER THE PARALLELOGRAM

Answers

1. Triangles *ABF* and *CDE* are equal (congruent).
2. The areas are the same.
3. Segment *BF* is longer than segment *AF*.
4. Rectangle *ACEF* has a lesser perimeter than parallelogram *BDEF*.
5. Answers will vary.

About the Problem

This problem is designed to further explore the idea that perimeters of a given area can vary.

Getting Started

Students should need no help with this problem, which is broken into simple steps for them on the worksheet.

Solutions

Problems 1 and 2: The triangles appear to be the same (congruent) and, therefore, their areas will be the same. We can think of "making the parallelogram out of the rectangle" by moving the triangle on the left to a new position on the right. Therefore, the area of the parallelogram will be the same as the area of the rectangle.

Problems 3 and 4: We can measure $\overline{BF}$ and $\overline{DE}$ to see that they are longer than $\overline{AF}$ and $\overline{CE}$. Therefore, the perimeter of the parallelogram is greater than that of the rectangle.

Problem 5: Students can easily do this by following the model they have just explored on the worksheet, varying the angles of the parallelogram and the lengths of the sides.

Going Beyond

Depending upon the ability level and background of your class, this problem could start a discussion that would reveal why the area of a parallelogram is determined by multiplying its *base* times its *altitude*.

PRIME TIME

A *prime number* is a number that can be divided evenly only by itself and by 1. The number 17 is an example of a prime number.

How many two-digit prime numbers can you write that use the digits 1, 2, 3, and 7? (Don't use any digit twice in the same number.)

Answer   13, 17, 23, 31, 37, 71, and 73

About the Problem

This problem introduces prime numbers. When you explain the definition of prime number, you may also want to define a nonprime as a *composite* number. The number 1 is neither prime nor composite.

Getting Started

You might suggest that students first list all possible combinations of two-digit numbers formed from 1, 2, 3, and 7, then test each of these numbers to learn which are prime.

Solution

A list of all possible combinations is given below:

12	not prime	(2 × 2 × 3)
13	prime	(1 × 13)
17	prime	(1 × 17)
21	not prime	(3 × 7)
23	prime	(1 × 23)
27	not prime	(3 × 3 × 3)
31	prime	(1 × 31)
32	not prime	(2 × 2 × 2 × 2 × 2)
37	prime	(1 × 37)
71	prime	(1 × 71)
72	not prime	(2 × 2 × 2 × 3 × 3)
73	prime	(1 × 73)

Going Beyond

One of the best activities when students are first working with prime numbers and factoring is the Sieve of Eratosthenes. This method goes back to ancient Greek arithmetic. To find which of the numbers from 1 to 100 are prime, we first eliminate all numbers that have a factor of 2 (except 2, which is prime). Next, we eliminate all numbers that have a factor of 3 (except 3, which is prime). We don't need

to eliminate numbers divisible by 4 or 6 since these were excluded at the same time we crossed out factors of 2. We need only eliminate prime factors up to 7. The next prime after 7 is 11, and dividing any two-digit number by eleven would result in a factor less than 11, which should already have been eliminated.

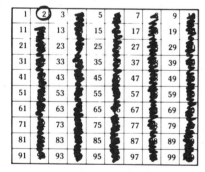

ELIMINATING MULTIPLES OF 2

ELIMINATING MULTIPLES OF 3

ELIMINATING MULTIPLES OF 5

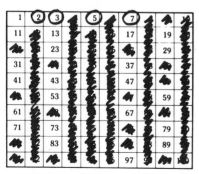

ELIMINATING MULTIPLES OF 7

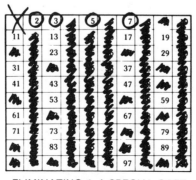

ELIMINATING 1, A SPECIAL CASE

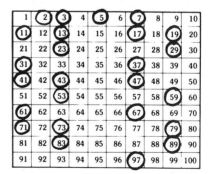

PRIME NUMBERS

If the digit sum of a number is divisible by 9, then the number itself is divisible by 9. For example, 495 is divisible by 9 because its digit sum (18) is divisible by 9. What other single digits have the same property?

Discussion for
DIVIDE AND CONQUER

Answer 1 and 3

About the Problem

This problem introduces a special property that all students should know as it is very helpful when factoring larger numbers.

Getting Started

Ask the students how they might organize a test for the other digits.

Solution

We approach this exploration by testing multiples of each single-digit number. As soon as we find *one* example that doesn't follow the rule, we can eliminate that number from consideration.

8 doesn't fit the rule since 32 (a multiple of 8) has a digit sum of 5, which is not divisible by 8.

7 doesn't fit the rule since 42 (a multiple of 7) has a digit sum of 6, which is not divisible by 7.

6 doesn't fit the rule since 36 (a multiple of 6) has a digit sum of 9, which is not divisible by 6.

5 doesn't fit the rule since 65 (a multiple of 5) has a digit sum of 11, which is not divisible by 5.

4 doesn't fit the rule since 28 (a multiple of 4) has a digit sum of 10, which is not divisible by 4.

3 does fit the rule.

2 doesn't fit the rule since 72 (a multiple of 2) has a digit sum of 9, which is not divisible by 2.

1 does fit the rule since any whole number is divisible by 1.

0 doesn't fit the rule since no number is divisible by 0.

Going Beyond

This problem is a natural introduction to the very useful tests for divisibility. Students have just learned the test for divisibility by 9, and have discovered a similar test for divisibility by 3. Ask them now to explore and devise tests for divisibility by 2, 4, 5, 6, and 10. A summary of these is as follows:

Rule for divisibility by 2: the last digit of the number is divisible by 2.

Rule for divisibility by 4: the number represented by the *last two digits* is divisible by 4.

Rule for divisibility by 5: the last digit is 0 or 5.

Rule for divisibility by 6: the number passes both divisibility test for 2 and 3.

Rule for divisibility by 10: the last digit is 0.

NOTE: These rules assume that the numbers are whole numbers.

Can the digits 1 through 9 be scrambled in such a way as to make a nine-digit number that is prime?

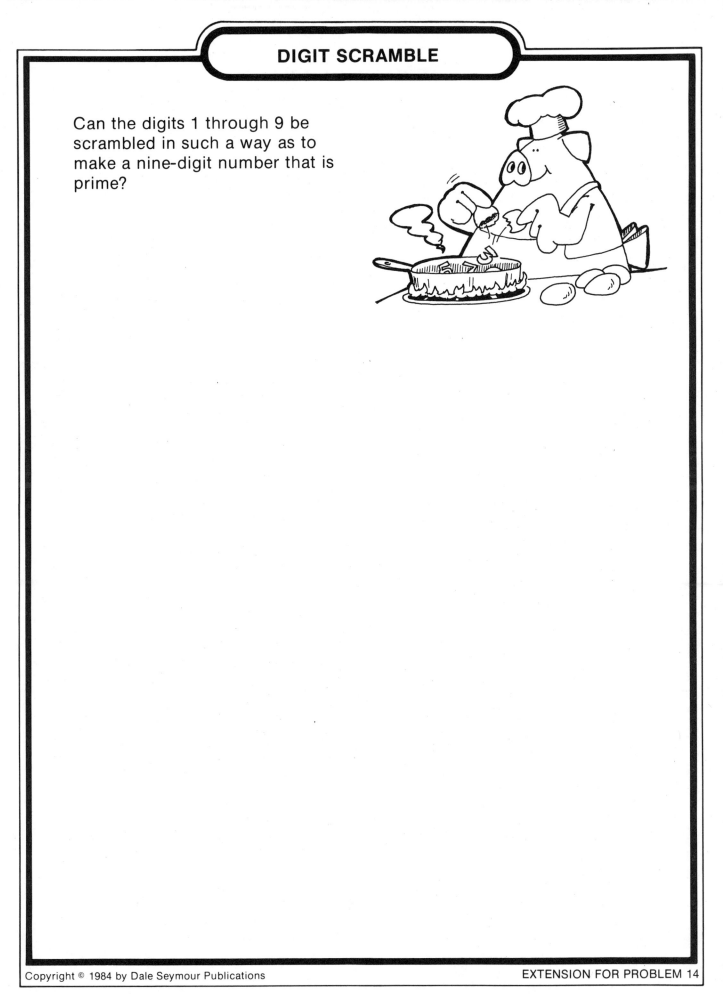

Discussion for
DIGIT SCRAMBLE

Answer No, it is not possible.

About the Problem

This problem initially seems to be very difficult, since there are 362,880 numbers to test. But with one simple test (*see Solution*), the answer is revealed. This problem vividly demonstrates the power of a single rule: using just one test of a known rule saves us from making over one-third of a million additional tests.

Getting Started

Students should not try this problem unless they know the tests for divisibility. However, avoid presenting this problem immediately following your discussion of the tests for divisibility, because the solution may then be too obvious.

Solution

The sum of the digits $(1 + 2 + 3 + 4 + 5 + 6 + 7 + 8 + 9)$ equals 45. This means that *any* arrangement of the digits will always be divisible by 9 and, therefore, the number can never be prime.

Going Beyond

Since this may be a very easy problem for some, try this as a follow-up problem:

What is the least number that is divisible by each of the numbers 1 through 10?

Answer: 2520

Solution: The number must have the following factors or combinations of factors: 2, 3, 4 (2×2), 5, 6 (2×3), 7, 8 $(2 \times 2 \times 2)$, 9 (3×3). However, we need not include all the listed factors. For example, we don't need *both* a factor of 4 and 8 since, if the number is divisible by 8, it will be divisible by 4 and 2. Therefore the answer is:

$$2 \times 2 \times 2 \times 3 \times 3 \times 5 \times 7 = 2520$$

BOX TALK

1. Which of the three boxes below can hold the most?

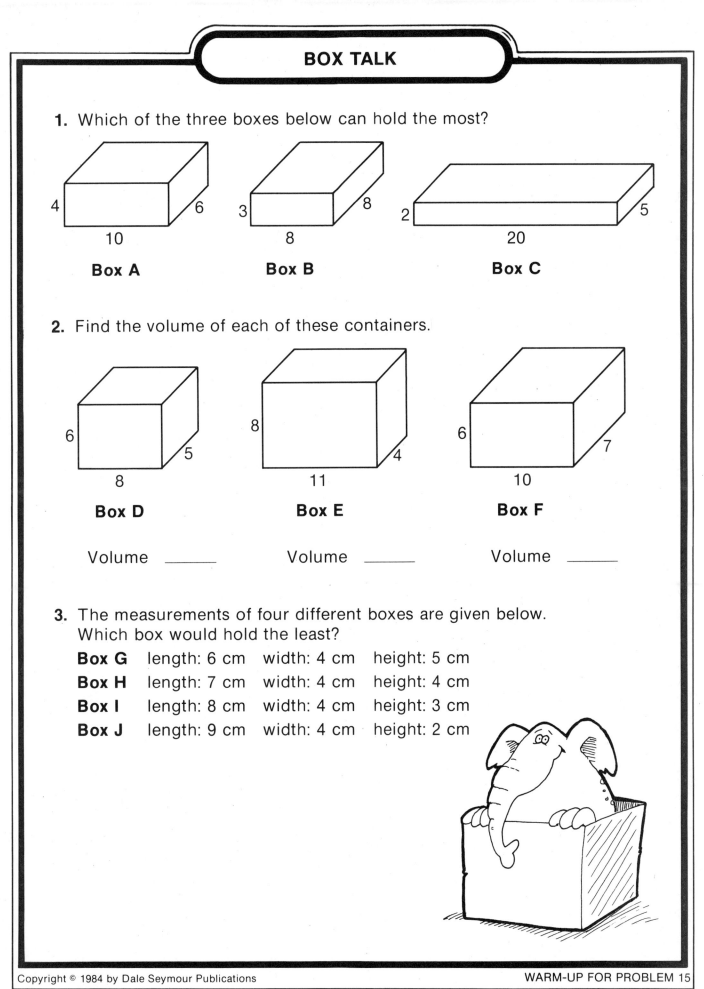

4   6
10
Box A

3   8
8
Box B

2   5
20
Box C

2. Find the volume of each of these containers.

6   5
8
Box D

8   4
11
Box E

6   7
10
Box F

Volume _____   Volume _____   Volume _____

3. The measurements of four different boxes are given below. Which box would hold the least?

Box G   length: 6 cm   width: 4 cm   height: 5 cm
Box H   length: 7 cm   width: 4 cm   height: 4 cm
Box I   length: 8 cm   width: 4 cm   height: 3 cm
Box J   length: 9 cm   width: 4 cm   height: 2 cm

WARM-UP FOR PROBLEM 15

BOX TALK

Answers

1. Box A (240 cubic units)
2. Box D: 240 cubic units
   Box E: 352 cubic units
   Box F: 420 cubic units
3. Box J (72 cubic units)

About the Problems

These problems involve an understanding of the concept of volume.

Getting Started

If students don't know the method for calculating the volume of a rectangular prism, you may need to do some readiness activities with wooden cubes before giving them this problem and the next two (*Zapper Holder* and *Blocks Box*).

Solutions

To calculate the volume of a rectangular prism (a box), we multiply its *length* times its *width* times its *height*. Or, $V = l \times w \times h$.

Going Beyond

Try the next problem, *Zapper Holder*.

Zappers come in a box that measures 2 by 4 by 8 units. Give the measurements of a larger box that would exactly hold 12 Zapper boxes.

ZAPPER HOLDER

Answers

There are 10 possible answers:

2 × 4 × 96	4 × 6 × 32
2 × 8 × 48	4 × 8 × 24
2 × 12 × 32	4 × 12 × 16
2 × 16 × 24	6 × 8 × 16
4 × 4 × 48	8 × 8 × 12

About the Problem

This problem concerns the concept of volume. It involves some visual thinking and can be extended to include the concept of factoring and making organized lists (see *Going Beyond*).

Getting Started

Students should be able to solve this problem without assistance. If they *do* need a hint, ask them how they might arrange the 12 smaller boxes to form a larger box.

Solution

The easiest approach is to imagine how twelve boxes might be arranged to form a rectangular prism. Students may need to make pencil sketches or use models to help them visualize such an arrangement. Note that models need not be to scale; we can even use cubes, just to get a certain configuration of boxes in mind. For example, we might stack them two deep, in two rows of three boxes each.

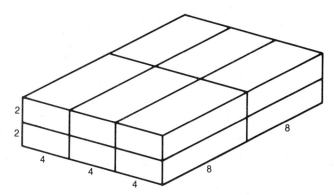

Once we have formed the larger box, we figure the measurements for each side by adding or multiplying those of each of the smaller boxes.

Height: 2 × 2 = 4
Length: 3 × 4 = 12
Width: 2 × 8 = 16

Going Beyond

The best extension for this problem is to find *all* possible larger cartons, as listed in the solution below. After suggesting this extension to the students and giving them plenty of time to work it out, plan to go through the solution carefully with them to clarify the organization of the procedure. That is, we consider the various arrangements of twelve boxes that would form a larger box (rectangular prism) by listing all possible configurations of the factors of 12, as shown in the chart.

NUMBER OF BOXES			RESULTING	
WIDE	DEEP	LONG	BOX DIMENSIONS	
1	1	12	2 × 4 × 96	
1	12	1	2 × 48 × 8	
12	1	1	24 × 4 × 8	
1	2	6	2 × 8 × 48	—duplicate
1	6	2	2 × 24 × 16	
2	1	6	4 × 4 × 48	
2	6	1	4 × 24 × 8	—duplicate
6	1	2	12 × 4 × 16	
6	2	1	12 × 8 × 8	
1	3	4	2 × 12 × 32	
1	4	3	2 × 16 × 24	—duplicate
4	3	1	8 × 12 × 8	—duplicate
4	1	3	8 × 4 × 24	—duplicate
3	1	4	6 × 4 × 32	
3	4	1	6 × 16 × 8	
2	2	3	4 × 8 × 24	—duplicate
2	3	2	4 × 12 × 16	—duplicate
3	2	2	6 × 8 × 16	—duplicate

Eliminating duplicates from the chart gives all possible answers.

Students may be interested to know that a Zapper manufacturer might go through this very process in determining the size of a shipping box for the product.

BLOCKS BOX

Give the dimensions of the smallest box that would exactly hold the following set of blocks.

NUMBER OF BLOCKS	NAME OF BLOCKS	DIMENSIONS
1	Big Cube	10 by 10 by 10
10	Flat Blocks	1 by 10 by 10
10	Rods	1 by 1 by 10
100	Little Cubes	1 by 1 by 1

Answer

Two possible answers are:
10 by 10 by 22
10 by 11 by 20

About the Problem

This problem requires students to combine their knowledge of volume and factoring; it involves a variety of problem-solving techniques.

Getting Started

Students should have the opportunity to think about this problem for a couple of days before you give any hints. Let them know that if an insight doesn't come to them, they can put the problem away and look at it again later.

Solution

One approach is to begin by finding the total volume of all the blocks (2200). Next, we can try to find what three factors of 2200 (length, height, and width) would accommodate all the blocks. Since the largest block is 10 by 10 by 10, each of the dimensions would have to be at least 10 units. If we assume that two of the dimensions are 10, then we can find that the third dimension is 22. (10 × 10 or 100 divides 2200 by 22.)

Alternatively, students might approach the problem visually, sketching the blocks to see how they might fit together to make a larger box. We start by sketching the one big cube, 10 × 10 × 10. Sketching the flat blocks, we see that they could be stacked beside the big cube to form an identical 10 × 10 × 10 figure. The ten rods could be placed side by side to form a single layer on top of the big cube. The hundred little cubes could fit together 10 × 10 to form a similar layer on top of the stacked flat blocks.

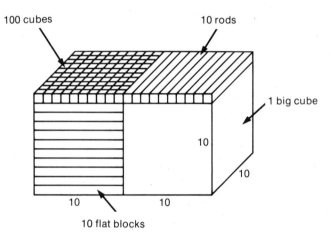

This way we have formed a rectangular prism; we simply add the measurements on each side to find the dimensions of the needed box:
10 × (10 + 1) × (10 + 10) = 10 × 11 × 20

Going Beyond

If you want to introduce a "real-world" element to this problem, explain to the class that, in actuality, the 100 cubes would probably be packaged loosely in a small plastic bag rather than being packed individually, as tightly as possible, into the larger carton. Also, packing cartons are available from box companies in standard sizes, which are more economical than custom-made boxes. The blocks manufacturer is more likely to choose a less expensive carton that is *close* to the appropriate size than to have one made up to fit the blocks exactly. In solving the problem, we found the *theoretical* minimum-sized box. If the information is available locally, some students might enjoy researching to find what standard-sized boxes would best hold the set of blocks, given the realities just mentioned.

CIRCULAR REASONING

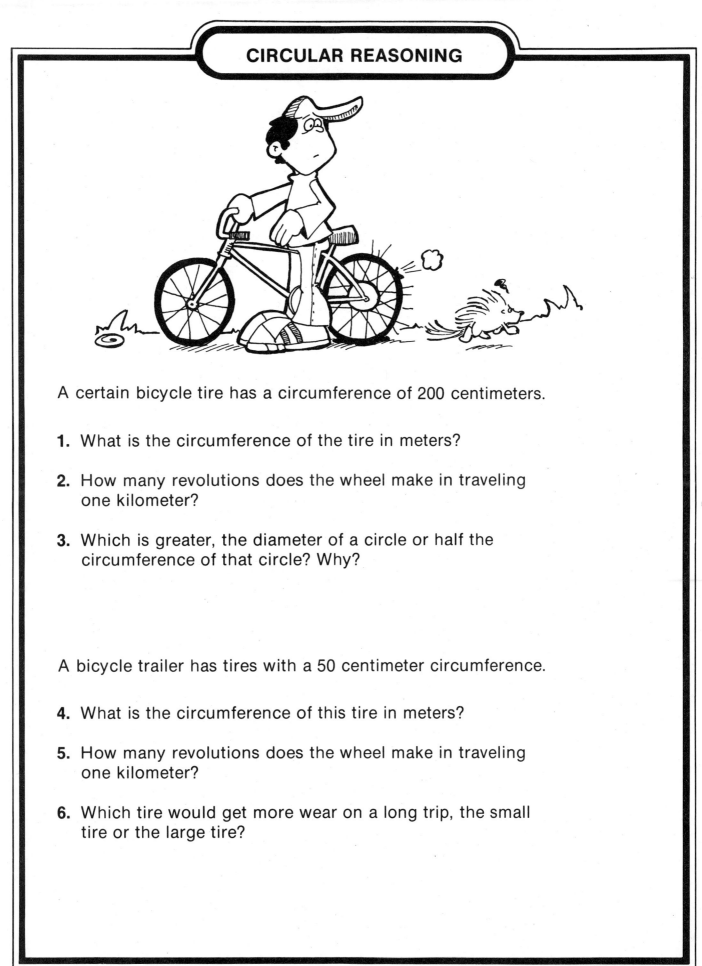

A certain bicycle tire has a circumference of 200 centimeters.

1. What is the circumference of the tire in meters?

2. How many revolutions does the wheel make in traveling one kilometer?

3. Which is greater, the diameter of a circle or half the circumference of that circle? Why?

A bicycle trailer has tires with a 50 centimeter circumference.

4. What is the circumference of this tire in meters?

5. How many revolutions does the wheel make in traveling one kilometer?

6. Which tire would get more wear on a long trip, the small tire or the large tire?

Discussion for
CIRCULAR REASONING

Answers

1. 2 meters
2. 500 revolutions
3. Half the circumference is greater than the diameter. The diameter represents the shortest distance between two points on the circle. Any other distance would be greater.
4. 0.5 meter
5. 2000 revolutions
6. The smaller tire would get more wear because it makes contact with the ground more often.

About the Problems

These questions are leading into important concepts about the relationships between diameter, radius, and circumference of a circle. They will be explored further in the next two problems *Record Performance* and *Call It Pi*.

Getting Started

You can help students understand the problem by using a circular object, such as a wastebasket rim, to show that one complete revolution establishes the length of the circle (circumference) as a length on a plane surface. This is the concept of the *trundle wheel*.

Solutions

1. 200 centimeters equal 2 meters by definition.
2. Since the tire moves 2 meters in one revolution, we divide 1 kilometer (1000 meters) by 2 meters, and the result is 500 revolutions.
3. This is easily seen by drawing a circle and a line that represents its diameter.
4. 50 centimeters equal one-half (0.5) meter by definition.
5. Following the same rationale as in problem 2: 1000 meters divided by 0.5 meter equals 2000 revolutions.
6. See answer.

Going Beyond

A natural extension of this activity is to have students make their own circular measurement instruments (trundle wheels). The device can be made with a stick for a handle and a circular disc (cardboard or wood) attached to the stick. A discarded wheel from home would be better yet. If you require students to cut a cardboard circular disc whose circumference is 1 meter or 1 yard, they will need to think about how that circular measurement could be made—a good exploration activity.

Suppose a 33-rpm record plays 20 minutes, and a 45-rpm record plays 5 minutes. How many more revolutions does the 33-rpm record make?

PROBLEM 16

RECORD PERFORMANCE

Answer   435 revolutions more*

About the Problem

Although most students are familiar with 33-rpm and 45-rpm records, few will have given much thought to the meaning of *rpm*, or *revolutions per minute*. This problem and the *Going Beyond* discussion should make students more aware of some properties of circles and concepts of rotation.

Getting Started

First, make sure that students understand what *rpm* means. For those who are stuck, the questions How many turns in one minute? two minutes? three minutes? and so on will probably reveal that the solution involves multiplication.

Solution

Multiplying 33 rpm times 20 minutes gives us the number of revolutions made by the long-playing record. 45 rpm times 5 minutes gives us the number of revolutions for the smaller record. To find the difference, we subtract:

    33 × 20 = 660
    45 × 5 = 225
    660 – 225 = 435 revolutions

Going Beyond

A good problem that will lead to an interesting discussion is as follows:

How *long* is the groove on one side of a 33-rpm record that plays 20 minutes?

Solution: We observe that there is one continuous groove on the record. We further observe that the part of the groove covered during one revolution gets smaller as the record plays.

One approach to the solution is to approximate the length of the groove covered in an *average* revolution. We would find such an average length by figuring the circumference midway through the wide ring of grooves. Since the record makes 660 revolutions from the beginning to the end of the groove, we can find the approximate length of the groove by multiplying 660 times the average length.

Our measurements of a typical 33-rpm record show a diameter of 21 cm or 8¼ inches midway through the grooves. $C = \pi d$, so the average circumference (length of one revolution) is about 70 cm or 26 inches.

    70 cm × 660 = 46,200 cm or 462 m
    26 inches × 660 = 17,160 inches or 1,430 feet

Another interesting question: How far does the needle move?

---

*Some students may know that a 33-rpm record technically makes 33⅓ revolutions per minute. We have ignored the fraction for the sake of simplifying the problem. If students use the fraction, their answer should be 441⅔ revolutions more.

CALL IT PI

Investigate the comparison between the lengths
(circumferences) of several circles and the lengths
of their diameters. Can you discover a relationship?

Circular object	Measure of circumference (C)	Measure of diameter (d)

What do you observe about the relationship between *C* and *d*?

_____

_____

EXTENSION FOR PROBLEM 16

CALL IT PI

Answer

In every case, the circumference of a circle is a little more than 3 times the diameter. More specifically, the answer is pi. The symbol for pi is π. Pi is an irrational number; the most commonly used rounded values of pi are 3.1416 or 22/7.

About the Problem

This is an investigation that every student should explore, as students are more likely to remember a concept that they discover on their own.

Getting Started

The chart on the worksheet will help students organize their listing of measurements. We intentionally did not include a column for the ratio relationships, so that students could discover that relationship themselves. Encourage the students to extend the chart however they like.

Solution

Students will discover that in each case, the circumference is about 3 times the diameter. After they have had an opportunity to discover this relationship or to record the specific ratio, ask students to calculate the ratio to one or two decimal places. A more accurate value of pi is 3.1415926535.

Going Beyond

Ask students to research the history of people's work with pi. How long has this relationship been known? Where did the symbol come from? How many decimal places of pi are known? Where else does pi appear in geometric relationships?